Dedication

I dedicate this book to my amazing friends and family, who have believed in me, been patient and understanding, have supported and encouraged me all along, and have tolerated all my weirdness: You know who you are and I love each and every one of you! To my parents, who without their amazing love and support, I would not be where I am today. To Mark (my husband): for all his love, support, and encouragement—thank you.

To my Grandmother, Mimi, who I cherish and miss: She brought to me the gift of books, and most importantly her love.

Author's Note

   Philadelphia has long been held as one of the most haunted cities within the United States. Sun-Ra was a Philadelphia native whose belief held that the city was, in fact, located within a spiritual nexus. This belief holds that this nexus holds an energy that allows spiritual energy to manifest. So it's no surprise that Philadelphia is host to many ghostly historical sites that have reports of spirit encounters. From Eastern State Penitentiary to Fort Mifflin, to mansions and cemeteries scattered throughout this beautiful city, and even the alleyways and back roads, there are spirits attempting to get our attention. Join us as we visit a few!

Philadelphia Haunts

At Eastern
State Penitentiary,
Fort Mifflin,
and Other
Ghostly Sites

Katharine Sarro

Schiffer
Publishing Ltd®

4880 Lower Valley Road, Atglen, Pennsylvania 19310

Designed by Stephanie Daugherty
Type set in :A Charming Font Expanded/
NewBskvll BT

ISBN: 978-0-7643-2987-6

Printed in China

Schiffer Books are available at special discounts for
bulk purchases for sales promotions or premiums.
Special editions, including personalized covers,
corporate imprints, and excerpts can be created
in large quantities for special needs. For more
information contact the publisher:

Published by Schiffer Publishing Ltd.
4880 Lower Valley Road
Atglen, PA 19310
Phone: (610) 593-1777; Fax: (610) 593-2002
E-mail: Info@schifferbooks.com

Please visit our web site catalog at
www.schifferbooks.com

We are always looking for people to write books on
new and related subjects. If you have an idea for a
book, please contact us at the above address.

This book may be purchased from the publisher.
Include $5.00 for shipping. Please try your
bookstore first. You may write for a free catalog.
In Europe, Schiffer books are distributed by:
Bushwood Books
6 Marksbury Ave.
Kew Gardens
Surrey TW9 4JF
England
Phone: 44 (0)208 392-8585
Fax: 44 (0)208 392-9876
E-mail: Info@bushwoodbooks.co.uk

Website: www.bushwoodbooks.co.uk
Free postage in the UK. Europe: air mail at cost.
Try your bookstore first.

Contents

Ackknowledgements

I would like to acknowledge the spirits of Philadelphia without whom there would no intriguing tales of ghostly encounters. I would like to thank Dinah Roseberry and Schiffer Books who have given me this incredible opportunity to write this book. I would like to thank Brett Bertolino for making our investigation at Eastern State Penitentiary possible, Lorraine Irby for setting up our investigation at Fort Mifflin, Wayne for guiding us through Fort Mifflin's intriguing history, Maureen Lynch for providing me with some fascinating information about the Academy of Music, a good friend of mine, Pete Hoge, for an amazing ghostly encounter on Camac Street, ECHO (East Coast Hauntings Organization) team members Christine Gentry-Rodriguez and Jack Rodriguez, Robbin Van Pelt of the United States Ghost Chasers, and our fine paranormal group CCPRS—Chester County Paranormal Research Society. Everyone who has told me their stories gets a big thank you, too! Those who have supported me, encouraged me, kept me grounded, and have indulged me in my fascination with paranormal phenomena: I appreciate all of your help—thank you.

Forward

The thriving American metropolis, Philadelphia, began as a small country town founded by William Penn in 1682, and went on to find itself at the forefront of the American Revolution and ultimately became the birthplace of America. "Philly," as we affectionately call it here in the City of Brotherly Love, is a remarkable place with a fascinating history.

It was here that the First Continental Congress took place at Carpenters' Hall. It was here that the fight for freedom was realized with the signing of the Declaration of Independence. It was here where our nation's forefathers converged for the Constitutional Convention. And it was Philadelphia that served as the nation's first capital.

While many cities boast about their "firsts," no American city can claim as many firsts as Philadelphia. Philadelphia was home to the nation's first public grammar school, botanical garden, university, public bank, stock exchange, mint, municipal water system, art school, art museum, zoo, public library, volunteer fire department, hospital and World's Fair. Nineteenth century Philadelphia was a magnet attracting many prominent American's and became the political and commercial epicenter of the young United States.

Today, Philadelphia is more than just cheese steaks and soft pretzels. Although it often gets a bad wrap it the

Eastern State Penitentiary at Night. Dramatic lighting illuminates the Eastern State Penitentiary's façade and half mile long 30-foot high wall. The award winning lighting design highlights the Penitentiary's forbidding façade every night. *Lighting design by The Lighting Practice. Photo by Tom Bernard.*

national media, Philadelphians like myself know that this is a city on the rise. At the turn of the twenty-first century, Philadelphia is experiencing unprecedented development, a restaurant renaissance, and a cultural rebirth. It is once again taking its place as one of America's premier cities.

The Kimmel Center for the Performing Arts now anchors the Avenue of the Arts on South Broad Street. The National Constitution Center and the new Liberty Bell Center have joined Independence Hall in an area of the city that has been dubbed "America's most historic square mile." The Barnes Foundation will soon open a new museum on the Benjamin Franklin Parkway and the Please Touch Museum will soon move to its new home in Memorial Hall, the last surviving major building from the 1876 Centennial Exposition. New skyscrapers tower over the statue of William Penn atop City Hall, although it remains the world's tallest masonry building. Three new state-of-the-art sports centers are now home to Philadelphia's four professional sports teams.

Historic Presence Rallies

Even as Philadelphia continues to grow, change and evolve, its greatest asset is still its history.

Today you can still go to the nation's first zoo or stroll down Elfereth's Alley, one of the oldest continuously occupied streets in America. You can explore dozens of historic landmarks like Independence Hall, Carpenters' Hall and Christ Church, where you can visit the graves of many early American leaders, including Benjamin Franklin. You can stop by Betsy Ross' house, where the first American flag was sewn or check out Bartram's Gardens, America's first botanical gardens. You can visit the Fairmount Water Works or take a tour of the Eastern State Penitentiary—both of these "must see" tourist destinations in the early nineteenth century, have once again opened their doors to tourists, this time as museums. Or you can travel a few minutes from downtown Philadelphia to Fort Mifflin and see the only completely intact Revolutionary War battlefield.

In Philadelphia you can step back in time, or so it seems.

All That and Haunted, Too

With such a rich history and so many historic structures still intact, it's no wonder that Philadelphia has a national reputation as one of America's most haunted cities. Both the Eastern State Penitentiary and Fort Mifflin have been the subject of paranormal investigations on the popular Sci-Fi Channel show, Ghost Hunters. In 2007, when the Travel Channel brought the UK's most popular paranormal investigation team to the United States for the first time, they decided to come to Philadelphia to conduct an unprecedented seven-hour live broadcast from Eastern State Penitentiary.

But is Philadelphia haunted?

That is a question you will ultimately have to answer for yourself. I invite you to visit this wonderful city through the pages of this book, and then pay a visit personally to experience the places firsthand and, in essence, step back in time.

—Brett Bertolino
Eastern State Penitentiary

Chapter One
Eastern State Penitentiary

2124 Fairmount Avenue
Philadelphia, Pennsylvania

The formidable presence of Eastern State Penitentiary looms like a gothic castle, complete with battlements, a tower, and even ivy-covered walls in the historic town of Philadelphia, just blocks away from the Philadelphia Museum of Art in Center City. It has a supernatural atmosphere which seems to permeate the property that covers twelve acres steeped in a sorted and infamous past. The once pristine, whitewashed walls and ceilings are now chipped and crumbling from the passage of time. A monstrous stone wall surrounds the perimeter of the penitentiary—a foreboding warning of what lurks amongst the confines within its walls.

This intimidating landmark is a place where, for more than a century, nobody wanted to go. Now, ironically, people are literally clamoring to get in! Once through the doors, and meandering about the prison, the cell blocks, the chapel, Death Row, the Guard Tower, and hospital, ones finds that all have an eerie feeling that fills the air. The walls have secret stories to tell.

There are rumors that there had been apparitions and specters within these cold stone fortress walls long before it ever closed for "business." In the 1970s, when the last living prisoners were shipped out of the prison, due to electrical and mechanical dysfunctions, and the guards had

completed their last rounds, a feeling of the preternatural filled the environment, creating a character of malice that would not soon leave.

The guards would speak to each other in hushed voices, and tell stories to anyone who would listen without thinking them crazed—they spoke to anyone who would listen to their chilling tales of the sounds of painful wailing, footsteps in the hallways, pacing within the walls of uninhabited cells, and unexplainable shadows darting about.

In the Beginning…

In 1822, construction began on the foundations and walls of Eastern State Penitentiary. It was built as an alternative to Philadelphia's Walnut Street Jail. The concept of the prison system was to reform the convicted, so that they would make peace with themselves and with their God. The system, devised by the Quakers, was designed to reform men. Unfortunately, the solitary confinement drove quite sane men to sheer madness.

This twelve-acre monstrous marvel of architecture was a tourist attraction even in 1836. Tourists would travel by horse and buggy just to get a look at the prison. The complex actually eclipsed Independence Hall as an attraction! Governments around the world visited the prison and based their own systems after Eastern State Penitentiary and their innovative methods. In fact, 300 prisons worldwide have based their designs on this political Philadelphia structure.

John Haviland created the original architectural concept and acted as the overseer of the construction of the

Interior of Eastern State Penitentiary. *Photo by Katharine Sarro*

penitentiary. The prison was designed so that the corridors formed spokes around a rotunda. The design allowed

the supervisors and guards to see every cell block, and absolutely no one could go unnoticed—not even the prison guards themselves.

On October 23rd, 1829, the Prison opened to its very first inmate, a burglar named Charles Williams. The prison was built with modern amenities, which included running water, central heat, state-of-the-art indoor plumbing, and skylights. Technically, Eastern State's inhabitants were blessed with comforts that many were going without at that time. Ironically enough, even President Andrew Jackson in the White House, did not yet have the modern amenity of central heat—in fact, he used coal burning stoves, and had no running water whatsoever.

Each prisoner was outfitted with a bunk, a Bible, a toilet, and a table.

Eastern State Penitentiary. *Photo by Katharine Sarro*

The prison was immaculate; each prisoner had his or her own private cell with a skylight referred to as "The Eye of God." Next to the cells was a private outdoor exercise yard sealed by a ten-foot wall.

When prisoners were brought into the prison, a black hood was placed over their heads, and they were led in and out of their cells with this hood. This was to ensure that they did not see the layout of the prison. It also discouraged inmates from attempting to dare an escape—and to keep the prisoners from seeing each other.

Communication between inmates was strictly forbidden; in fact the penalties were severe.

The Iron Gag: This punishment was considered to be the deadliest and was used on those who did not obey the law of *no communication*. An iron collar was clamped onto the tongue and then chained to his or her wrists, which were then strung up high behind the back. Any movement resulted in the tearing and bleeding of the inmate's tongue. Most inmates died from this punishment due to the loss of blood—it was a cruel method of torture.

The Water Bath: Any prisoner who broke the rules risked being doused with cold water and hung from a wall for an evening. This was a popular form of punishment during the winter months. Often, the inmates were covered with a layer of ice over their skin by the morning.

The Mad Chair: A good reason for the name of this punishment— those that endured it literally went mad. The inmates were strapped in so tightly to a chair with leather straps that is was absolutely impossible for them to make any movement whatsoever. The prisoners would sit for days, without food, until the circulation in their bodies practically stopped.

The Hole: It was a pit dug in the ground under Cell Block 14. This is where incorrigible men were thrown in and locked up for weeks at a time. They would be slung a single slice of bread, but they would be lucky if they grabbed it before the rats and roaches got to it.

These harsh forms of punishment were not devised by the Quakers in the name of reform. The punishments were actually created by the hired staff in the prison. Before its reform in 1913, the prison, which was designed to house 250 prisoners, held 1,700 inmates, all crammed into tiny cells with little light and poor ventilation. The solitary system was officially abandoned in 1913, and was then run as a congregate prison until the doors closed. All prisoners were evacuated in the early 1970s.

The *Get Out of Philadelphia* Card

There were a number of escapes from Eastern State Penitentiary; the most notable was actually planned by a plaster worker by the name of Clarence Klinedinst and his cellmate William Russell. The two cellmates of Cell Block 7 dug into their wall and managed to dig fifteen feet down and a total of ninety-seven feet out to Fairmount Avenue. Twelve prisoners escaped and found themselves on the corner of 22nd and Fairmount Avenues. (Imagine a beautiful Sunday morning on April 3, 1945, when, all of a sudden, men wearing prison garb are scattered and running amongst the church-going crowd!)

All twelve men scattered, but the notorious bank robber, "Slick Willie Sutton," was captured within minutes. The funny thing was that one prisoner, James Grace, actually returned to the prison, rang the doorbell, and asked if he could come back in because he was hungry!

The very first escape from the Penitentiary was in 1832, by prisoner number 94; William Hamilton dared to escape the confines by scrambling down from the warden's quarters. In 1923, Leo Callahan scaled the east wall with five other inmates. Leo Callahan is still at large, and authorities remain in search of his whereabouts to this day.

The inmates who have resided within the boundaries of the prison have intriguing stories to tell as well; some say (as you will hear more about shortly!) that Capone was visited by the "ghosts" of those he had killed.

...Not So Bad...

Interestingly, some of the inmates who last lived in Eastern State Penitentiary were actually quite fond of their time within the prison. Apparently, the guards were relatively relaxed and would take the time to talk to the prisoners. A common phrase used was "take a laxative!" This meant, go lie down and relax, chill out a bit.

The prisoners were not allowed the use of playing cards, so instead, they used dominos. They often played poker with the dominos, and their "money" was their cigarettes. In fact, there were footlockers full of cigarettes.

Some of the prisoners had plants in their small windows—though this is quite different from the trees which have now taken over some of the cells. One inmate accounts, in *Voices of Eastern State*, that he had actually grown a huge *pot* plant. The ironic thing was that he says that none of the guards ever seemed to be aware, or care, that he had this monstrous marijuana plant in his cell! Although the conditions of Eastern State Penitentiary were poor, some spirits stayed "high."

...But Worse...

Charles Dickens gives account, after his 1842 visit to the prison, in Chapter Seven of his travel journal,

American Notes for General Circulation. The chapter is titled, "Philadelphia and its Solitary Prison."

> "In its intention I am well convinced that it is kind, humane, and meant for reformation; but I am persuaded that those who designed this system of Prison Discipline, and those benevolent gentleman who carry it into execution, do not know what it is that they are doing...I hold this slow and daily tampering with the mysteries of the brain to be immeasurably worse than any torture of the body; and because its ghastly signs and tokens are not so palpable to the eye, ...and it extorts few cries that human ears can hear; therefore I the more denounce it, as a secret punishment in which slumbering humanity is not roused up to stay."

By 1970, the electrical and mechanical systems within Eastern State were in horrible shape, and inmates were sent to the State Correctional Institution at Graterford. The doors were officially closed in 1971. In the early 70s to mid 80s, the prison was all but abandoned, and instead of housing inmates, it became the home of stray cats and trees rooted within the cells.

In 1974, Mayor Frank Rizzo suggested demolishing Eastern State so that a criminal justice center could be constructed. Fortunately, this suggestion was not heeded.

An Escape From Demolition

It was in 1988 that the Eastern State Task Force convinced Mayor Goode to urge the Redevelopment Authority to reject all proposals for the commercial use of Eastern State. This group of historians, preservationists, and architects, known as the Eastern State Task Force, began showing small tours of the prison. In 1991, Pew Charitable Trusts funded the preservation and stabilization efforts of Eastern State Penitentiary.

Through the years, the ominous structure of Eastern State has attracted a great deal of attention in the media. It has been used in videos and in movies, such as the Dead Milkmen's video for "Punk Rock Girl" and the blockbuster movie, *12 Monkeys,* staring Brad Pitt, Bruce Willis, and Madeline Stowe. MTV's show, *Fear,* filmed a paranormal investigation within the eerie walls of Eastern State. The Sci-Fi channel's *Ghost Hunters* investigation scared the guys so much, you hear one of them scream, "Dude Run!" The TAPS investigation revealed a walking specter in Cell Block 12 on their TV show, *Ghost Hunters.* CNN, The History Channel, The Discovery Channel, BBC, and even The Food Network's *Emeril Live*, have all filmed within the walls of Eastern State Penitentiary.

The Travel Channel's *Most Haunted* did a live program within the decaying prison that lasted overnight. There were some interesting points in the show that brought back harrowing memories of our own night there! Yvette, one of the show's investigators, asked the spirits to tap out how many spirits were surrounding them—and the tapping totaled up to fifteen taps! Upon entering one of the cells, a large metal washer fell down right next to the visitors. In yet another cell, a table moved on its own, and another washer fell. This was all in the first four hours of the program!

To add to the media exposures, ESP has created a fun side to the paranormal influx sweeping the nation. Each fall, "Terror Behind the Walls" fills Eastern State Penitentiary's cells and is by far one of the best haunted locations and attractions for a truly frightening haunted house. But don't take *my* word for it! It holds the title of "One of America's Scariest Halloween Attractions" as noted by the *Travel Channel*.

One of the most notorious inmates of Eastern State was Al Capone. He served eight months of a year sentence at Eastern State Penitentiary when picked up on a concealed weapons charge. It was here that he shared his fine wines with the Warden.

He was placed in a lavish cell fit for a king; it was quite different from the other inmate "quarters." The Public Ledger on August 20, 1929 reported:

> "The whole Room was suffused in the glow of a desk lamp which stood on a polished desk. ...The once-grim walls of the penal chamber hung tasteful paintings, and the strains of a waltz were being emitted by a powerful cabinet radio receiver of handsome design and fine finish..."

It is said that, while serving his sentence, he was visited by the ghosts of those he had killed. One of them was James Clark, one of The Saint Valentines Day Massacre victims. Inmates reported that they could hear Capone yelling, begging, and crying for "Jimmy" to leave him alone. Capone was so convinced that Clark's spirit was plaguing him, that he eventually contacted a psychic to rid himself of the angry ghost.

Capone's own personal valet recounted a time when he says he came across the spirit of Clark standing near a window of Al Capone's apartment. It is said that the vengeful ghost of James Clark followed Capone from Eastern State Penitentiary until his dying day.

A Prison Visit

As a paranormal investigator, I am enthralled and amazed by this humungous prison and its ghostly inhabitants, and now, finally, I am doing a paranormal

Al Capone's cell in Eastern State Penitentiary. *Photo by Katharine Sarro*

investigation within the walls of one of the most notoriously haunted buildings in the city of Philadelphia.

It is November 11, 2006. Yes, 11/11 a good lucky number, so I know we will have some amazing experiences. As we begin our investigation, I am clamoring to retain some sense of maturity instead of acting like an eight year old! When hunting ghosts as a kid, I would run around with bailing twine, scissors, sometimes a tree branch, tape, and M&M's™. I had no idea what I would do if I found a ghost at my young age—feed it M&M's? Tie it up? I knew I could get a fingerprint from tape and that was about it!

Now, many years later, I am equipped with the proper tools. I have my new fancy EOS camera, an analog recorder, a flashlight, and most importantly, what I like to call "the *Scooby Doo* mentality." I want to remain skeptical and debunk any phenomenon before jumping to any ghostly conclusions.

It is slightly chilly, so my hands shake a bit with the cold and with my building excitement. Having broken into two teams for investigative purposes, my group proceeds to walk through the dark corridors, well armed with different tools. Truly working as a crack team, one investigator logs date, time, and temperature; one takes video; a few use cameras (digital and 35mm); others employ a digital compass or EMF (electromagnetic field) detector, and/or audio recording devices. One of my teammates uses my digital recorder, since I've run out of hands and pocket space. (I wish I could design a garment to house all of these contraptions!)

My cargo pants feel a little loaded down with all of the gear and there are puddles from the rain. Of course, I step in some watery spots. Now I'm a mess, the bottoms of my pants, because I'm loaded down with gear, are soaked. I bend down and say, "Sorry, that's me squishing!" (All sounds have to be identified in this kind of environment, including any mistakes we make!) I quickly roll up my pants a bit.

There has been some recent rain, so as we walk along inside the old structure, we hear the trickle of water. This only adds to the already-spooky atmosphere.

As I peek inside one of the cells, I could swear I see a shadow at the corner of the cell, so I quickly take a photo. But that's not the only shadow in the building. I keep seeing them darting around, like they are going from cell to cell. Unnerving.

At the end of one of the cell blocks, my whole team comes to a stop. We stay very quiet and still—someone is whispering, but who? It is no one in our group—we are the *only group* in Cell Block 12 right now—so who do we hear?

We decide to do some EVP work. Maybe the spirits will talk with us. The Electronic Voice Phenomenon (EVP) is not audible to our naked ears; this phenomenon is only audible through means of a recording device. So we stopped and asked a few questions to our hushed whispers in hopes that some answers will be caught on tape.

Author Tidbit!

One of my funny experiences: We were standing in one of the old prison showers when, suddenly, soap dropped to the floor. I laughed nervously and said, "Don't drop the soap!" My teammates laughed, I felt someone slap my backside, and I turned to see which of our investigators had playfully hit me. But no one was there! Spirits do have a sense of humor sometimes!

There were times during the investigation when I felt chills on my neck, as if someone was tickling me, and even a tug on the braids of my hair. I felt a cold wind pass by my ears that sounded like a whisper, offering to, "meet me here…" I remember thinking, *Where? When? Who are you? What do you want? Are you a prisoner? A Guard? A Warden?* I wanted to go into each cell and find my whispering friend. I never found him, but maybe he was the one I caught in an EVP saying, "pssst, pssst," in Cell Block 12.

Dinah, an investigator on one team that evening, told me, "It was very strange to me that, though the room temperatures in the prison were not significantly cold, it felt *extremely* cold. Most of us talked of cold hands, noses, and such. I chose to put on a coat after the first cell block investigation. It was warmer outside, with the same temperature readings, then it was inside."

EVPs were many this night. Another one we caught on tape is a whisper: "Check it out…" This was taken from Cell Block 12, too.

I bravely climbed all the way up the Guard Tower; I was shaken by climbing upwards because I have a nervousness of heights—so I was freaked out to say the least. The weird thing was, after I had made the climb and was looking at the night sky, I felt as if an arm held me back against the wall up there. It was an amazing sight, the lights of the City of Philadelphia, overlooking the twelve acres of this gigantic prison; it was an absolutely incredible vision. But invisible arms held me back (in safety?)…that was incredible as well.

Some Preliminary Creepiness

We found some compelling evidence amongst all of our recordings. But this was not an investigation where leaving the premises and pouring over collected data was the only source of paranormal activity. Oh no! Our paranormal researchers had some… interesting… accounts of what happened to them during our investigation.

One investigator reported that, as he was walking, it felt as if fingers were reaching past the bars and grabbing out at him. We conducted an EVP session in Cell Block 12 to try to hear the voices of the past. During our session, we all heard something stirring at the end of the hallway and even saw a shadow move about. The EVPs, "psst, psst," and the whispered "check it out," mentioned earlier sounded very out of place amongst our normal voices.

In Cell Block 4, I had an overwhelming sense of sadness, and tears formed quickly in my eyes. Another of our investigators said, "I cried the whole time in Cell Block 4, and I just don't know why!"

I stopped abruptly in front of a cell in this area and heard a distinct cry of agony. We conducted some EVP work and I conversed with our sad "inmate." We all stood paralyzed with intrigue and excitement. After we had concluded our EVP session, we all felt a sudden cold breeze fly and push past us. I was so exhilarated and so were my teammates.

Later, as we began to go through evidence, we became aware of how fortunate and incredible our findings were. While in Cell Block 4, during an EVP session, there is a deep sigh of a man heard after the question, "What year were you brought here?" At another cell, I asked questions about prison food and asked if the inmate missed his mother's cooking. After I posed the question, "Are you missing home?" a male voice says, "I am."

One team member captured, on video, the jingle of keys and the sound of footsteps walking up and down the cell block, though neither incident had visibly shown—no keys, no walking feet. Mind you, the camera was left running while investigators were not currently in that cell block. Quite often when we investigate, we leave a camera running in an unoccupied space. The footsteps sound as if they walk directly behind the camera and then walk down the hallway, just out of sight.

We investigated whether anyone had been in the vicinity of that corridor, and were assured that no one had been. In fact, all of our teams were split into smaller ones and occupying very different sections of the prison at the time the video footage was taken.

Another investigator told me that he had gone, alone, into one of the cells and, as he had turned to leave, he was pushed quite abruptly. No one was there to push him. He was shoved so hard that he banged his head on the wall of the cell and was significantly hurt by the incident.

The way the cells are built, the doorway is small, and then the cell itself has a high ceiling. Back in the day, the prisoners were (as I mentioned before) hooded when brought outside their cells so they could not see anything or anyone around them. The guards would bend the prisoners' heads downward so they would not bang their heads on the way in or out of the cells. The "head pusher" in this case, was not so careful with our investigator. (I should note here, that though intriguing, ghost investigations can become hazardous if one is not very, very careful.)

There is a chapel located in the Penitentiary that has some chipped fragments of beautiful mural paintings. As we walked into the chapel, we smelled something really odd—and quite horrible. Was it possibly a dead rat, a bad case of flatulence, or maybe something more sinister? Absolutely *no one* 'fessed up" to any gaseous emissions… And we knew that the ESP staff were vigilant when it came to the grounds. Still, we were wary as we moved along.

As we continued our investigation, we looked all over for dead rodents or some reason for the smell—not that I really wanted to find a varmint of any kind, since I am usually rather squeamish about dead, smelly, decaying things. (Ghosts are one thing, decaying carcasses, quite another.) I was relieved to *not* find a stinky rat, however, a bit unsettled by a weird feeling of being watched. What was going on in this supposed place of worship?

Some of our members felt a bit uneasy, so we decided to quietly recite the *Lord's Prayer*. The odd—but good—thing was, after reciting the prayer, we noticed that the stench had lifted and had mysteriously gone away.

East Coast Hauntings Organization Joins the Chester County Paranormal Research Society

ECHO—www.ghostecho.com
CCPRS—www.chestercountyprs.com

We invited two guest investigators from East Coast Hauntings Organization to come along with us on this prison journey. Christine Gentry-Rodriguez and Jack

Rodriguez of ECHO made some amazing discoveries when going through their evidence.

Christine is the Founder and Director of East Coast Hauntings Organization (ECHO) and is aided in her paranormal research with intuitive abilities, which define paranormal areas more easily and are used to enhance scientific documentation. Jack is a computer engineer with a leading software development company and has a wide range of skills, often applied to the field of paranormal photography and data collection. He's currently working on new techniques for studying anomalies via the modification of standard field equipment, such as infrared photography and digital 3D photo imaging of paranormal events. These were great professionals to add to our teams for this most creepy investigation.

After our night at Eastern State, Chris was kind enough to send me her written report of their findings. So read carefully—it's chilling.

The Technical Side of Ghost Hunting at ESP

Christine reports from an ECHO Investigation document: I am the founder of ECHO and also a clairsentient and intuitive. Jack is clairvoyant. Along with these abilities, we also use the usual ghost hunting equipment along with some high-tech, experimental equipment such as a professionally converted digital Infrared SLR camera and 3D digital imaging camera set-ups.

We have discovered that there is a good chance of getting better documentation and increasing potential paranormal contact when we use our personal sensitivities to locate hot spots and then document heavily in these areas with scientific equipment. The idea is to draw entities to us so they can be photographed or evaluated with calibrated equipment more efficiently and effectively.

Using scientific equipment, the two of us were in one of two teams split up to investigate Cell Blocks, 4, 7, and 12. We also walked quickly through Cell Block 9, the Guard Tower, and outside the grounds, around or inside various maintenance buildings, the hospital, and exercise yards.

Cell Block 4

Scientific Research:

Cell block 4 is considered one the best areas to investigate for paranormal activity, specifically its propensity to have continual and unexplained temperature variations. Cold spots abound here. They may be stationary for long periods of time or roving about. The cold spots are often simultaneous with unexplained electromagnetic readings.

During our investigation, we had several such occurrences. About halfway down the long corridor of cells, with doors aligned across from each other, we felt the first cold spot, which had a limited area size of about six feet by five feet. I felt the cold spot, along with several others near cell number 632.

The ambient temperature was 64.1 degrees F. and did not appear to register the extreme cold some of us were feeling. The baseline EMF reading for the block was around .1 to .2 milligauss. During this event, Mark's EMF meter read between 1.5 and 2.3 milligauss. At one point, Kyle mentioned that his ears felt pressurized, as if they were about to pop, like they might on an airplane when air pressure increases around you during an altitude climb.

The most interesting event in Cell Block 4 happened at the far end of corridor near an exit door. The last four doors near the end of the block, and farthest from the central hub where we entered, were abnormally cold.

Our breath could be seen at times in the corridor. If we popped out heads into an open cell door and exhaled, we could definitely see our breath as well. Certain cells near the end exit exhibited these cold phenomena while others just a few feet back did not. The ambient temps registered at 64.1 degrees, but it was obvious that it felt much lower than that to our chilled bodies.

We have no explanation for these phenomena. However, when I asked the security person standing nearby about the extreme cold variation, she replied that it always occurs only in the far end of the Cell Block, which was reopened in 1971. I was also told that these first floor cells were considered the "punishment block," while the upper floor gallery was for woman prisoners. A punishment block was meant to be a total isolation zone for prisoners. The cells had no furniture, and contact with other people was forbidden.

This area served as extreme deprivation quarters for all prisoners sent here. For years, they lived devoid of human contact and basic physical comforts. The only link to the outside world were thin, open ceiling slivers with bars called "The Eye of God" where prisoners were instructed to contemplate on their past misdeeds for years on end. Snow, rain, and freezing temperatures entered the cells as well.

The second to the last cell on the left side proved to be the most interesting of all. We recorded an EMF reading starting at .7 milligauss and continually rising to 1.2 milligauss directly in the open door way upon my request that anyone there, get closer to my meter and make it rise so we'd know somebody was really there.

The cold coming through the cell door toward us in the hallway was extreme. Dinah, who stood next to me in the tiny opening, felt the cold as well as she recorded the rising EMF meter readings. At the same time, Dinah suddenly started to cry for no reason. She said that she felt very sad and depressed and had never had such an experience before in her life. Soon after the energy dissipated.

We gathered together and did a quick EVP session by being very quiet and asking questions with pauses afterwards. The idea is to initiate a verbal response from any nearby entities, which might be recorded on the tapes. At one point, Kyle claimed that something might have touched his forehead. Jack mentioned that he felt that someone had come up behind us. Afterwards, we left the cellblock.

Intuitive Research:

Sensitives encountered several anomalous energies in Cell Block 4. I felt what I classify as a male energy within ten minutes of walking into the block. This was near a left-hand cell about a third of the way down the hallway.

Soon, the energy around me, along with a cold spot, dissipated and I walked down the block only to encounter another energy spot. At the same time, Kyle felt another cold spot near a cell across from me. This is when I called Mark over with his EMF meter and it registered a 2.3 milligauss reading. This second energy I felt was also a possible male entity.

We continued toward the end of the block and encountered an abnormal freezing coldness. I was inexplicably drawn toward the second from the last cell on the left-hand side of the block, very near the exit door. I felt a male energy in the doorway and called Dinah over to feel it and the cold coming out of the cell. She felt the freezing temperature as well.

As we stood there, I took EMF readings and requested that the male energy I felt should try to make the device click louder. At that point, the meter readings rose steadily from .7 milligauss to 1.2 milligauss. This high-energy reading was held maintained for some time before dissipating. It was during this experience in front of door that Dinah began to cry. Perhaps she was picking up on the distressed and despairing state of a male entity.

Around this same time, Jack described a man wearing a jumpsuit being in the area as seen by his mind's eye [this is one way Jack's sensitive works]. The inmate number 6537 comes to him, along with a vision of his head features. The prisoner had a receding hairline along the sides and forehead with otherwise, short dark and wavy hair.

The most validating event of the evening for me was my talk with the [live] security guard after the paranormal event in the cell doorway occurred. Besides explaining how the cells in that area were used as punishment cells, the female guard also confided in me that she'd had a paranormal experience relating to that very cell door which she'd never told anyone before.

The guard explained that one night she'd come down on her rounds to check Cell Block 4. When she reached a spot near the last four cells, she was startled to see a black man stoop his head and walk out of the second from the last cell on the left side, move straight across the corridor, and stoop to enter the opposite cell door, and then disappeared.

She couldn't believe her eyes. Nor could she believe what she'd seen as I purposely walked to that very same cell and stated that a man's energy was occupying that cell doorway during the investigation.

While we did an EVP session before leaving the block, Kyle felt that someone had touched his forehead and Jack believed that a man had walked up behind the group. He also thought that this man was someone who "controlled the cell block" while alive and still believed that he was in charge of the area. During the EVP session, I asked the question, "What do you fear the most?" I got the mental answer, "loneliness."

Cell Block 12

Scientific Research:

Cell Block 12 was the most interesting area we investigated all night. Like Cell Block 4, this block had two levels. We went directly upstairs to investigate. On the upper floor, we were forced to walk in single file down the long cell block via a right-hand catwalk.

Within a short period of time, we encountered some cold spots of short duration in front of several of the open cell doors. Again, the air around these areas felt extremely cold, but did not register on the digital thermometer as anything but a range of 64.1 degrees F. One of these cold spots was near the seventh door down on the right.

As the group reached a point halfway down the right catwalk, an EVP (Electronic Voice Phenomena) session was held. We all stopped and Kyle did some taps on the railing to see if anything unseen would answer. It was common for prisoners to signal if they were entering or leaving a cell by a series of raps. Kyle tapped twice on the catwalk railing, but there were no responses.

After this, we continued down to the right side end of the cellblock. The last room on this side was a large eight foot by ten foot. Mark and I were the first to enter the tiled room. We got halfway inside when Mark's Walkie on his hip burst out with a male voice and white noise. He picked it up, thinking it was the other team in another area of the prison contacting him. He answered the call, but no one responded.

As soon as he re-clipped the Walkie on his hip, the device made a weird squeak and crackle noise before stopping. About this time, I felt a male energy. Then the Walkie squeaked and buzzed again. It occurred to us that something in the shower might be activating the Walkie. We began to encourage contact by requesting any spirits to keep activating it. There were no other chirps from the speaker despite our requests; however, the physically-felt electromagnetic energy inside the shower was intense.

Jack entered the shower at that point and we located the energy in the rear right corner of the shower. Soon after, a cold spot developed in that corner and Mark complained that he felt a pressure behind his eyes while Jack mentioned that he was freezing beside that corner area.

We studied the corner spot with an EMF meter and a digital thermometer, but got insignificant readings. Again, the paranormal activity was felt by investigators, but not registering. After thirteen minutes in the stall, the cold spot and energy dissipated completely. The three of us left the shower, and other investigators went in.

The only paranormal response others got in the shower happened to Kyle. He was startled when something pushed him out of the shower as he was exiting. He was the last person to leave and felt a strong push on his back from behind. He was quite startled by it and didn't want to return into it alone.

Because of the activity, we decided to remain in that area and do a tapping response session. Kyle hit the catwalk railing two times and one minute later, everyone heard two taps in response far down the catwalk. Kyle tapped three times again and we received two distinct taps in answer. A third time, Kyle tapped out two more taps and a two-tap response was received in another minute.

Encouraged, it was decided that Mark and Jack would return to the stairs far down the catwalk and listen to see if they could hear the taps down there. When Jack and Mark were in position far away, Kyle and I went into the shower stall. We wanted to see if banging from inside a room would make any difference.

Kyle tapped twice very loudly on an interior shower pipe. One minute after Kyle tapped, two answering taps occurred somewhere down and in the vicinity of the middle of the catwalk. No one else was on the upper floor with our team members and the security guard was visible about twenty feet away.

We repeated this tapping experiment again. Kyle hit the shower pipe two times and a minute later, two responding taps occurred somewhere down the length of the catwalk away from us and toward the stair entrance to our left side. Kyle again hit the shower pipe three times and Mark's radio immediately crackled and squeaked so we started over. Kyle tapped two times. A minute and half later, two taps were heard in response. Kyle tapped once more and two weak taps were heard almost two minutes later.

We moved to the left catwalk and continued with another tapping session. However, after five failed attempts to illicit a response, we continued down the left side catwalk toward the stairs.

We eventually returned to a first group of cells up from the stair landing and encountered a couple of cold spots that dissipated very quickly. After reaching Mark and Jack near the stairs, Jack informed us that he'd seen a blue, grapefruit-sized orb fly by very near to them and across a left side window adjacent to the stairway.

Most interesting was the fact that both Mark and Jack claimed they never heard the response taps that the rest of the team heard at the opposite end of the cell block near the shower. This could indicate that the taps were actually very close to the main group and their location was being distorted by the acoustics inherent to a large open cell block.

Intuitive Research:

From my standpoint, the best paranormal interaction with spirit occurred in the shower on Cell Block 12. Both Jack and I experienced the cold spot and the strong, vibrant male energy associated with the far right corner of the tiled room.

I immediately sensed that a male often stayed in the shower stall and was very depressed and distressed. I also felt that he'd been traumatized in that area, possibly losing his life there at an age somewhere in his early twenties. I also got the name, "Johnny" very clearly when trying to communicate with him. Jack picked up the name "Bobby."

Jack saw clairvoyantly that the brown-haired man in the corner was extremely upset and crouching naked there. It was unclear what had happened to him, though an EVP recording discovered much later, obtained while we were talking to the man, leads us to conclude that he was beaten while in the shower.

Cell Block 7
Scientific Research:
For our group, not much paranormal activity occurred in this cell block. The ceilings were extremely high and that may have inhibited our ability to get EMF meter documentation or variant temperature readings. In general, paranormal activity appeared to decline from this point on (after 2:30 am) throughout the prison.

Intuitive Research:
There was one interesting experience in this cell block. Soon after we entered, Jack said that he saw a man standing on the left side of the upper catwalk who was trying to get our attention from the second-floor gallery. The catwalk in this more modern building consisted of a narrow horseshoe-shaped walkway that hugged the exterior walls and was bordered by a low iron railing. The middle of the upper floor was completely open to the ceiling, unlike the other cellblocks we investigated.

Jack described the middle-aged man as wearing tan pants and a white shirt. The man also has a receding hairline on the sides and front, and short, dark wavy hair. He is unsure if this was an inmate. It's possible the man could have been a guard. I asked the man to come down because we couldn't get up there, and an intensely cold energy enveloped the group. Many of us took photos up toward the catwalk during this event.

A shot taken during our investigation on November 11, 2006. An orb situated high above the crew seems to have a face embedded. *Photo courtesy of Christine Gentry-Rodriguez*

A close up of the orb has clear features. *Photo courtesy of Christine Gentry-Rodriguez*

I took photos with a specially converted digital camera that allows only infrared light (IR) to filter through the lens. I took several photos upwards toward the catwalk when Jack said a man was standing up there and got one IR photo that was quite interesting. In that picture, the group is looking upwards at the catwalk. There is an orb above the group and then another circular anomaly very high up and closer to my lens. This anomaly contains a bizarre human face, very gaunt and ghoulish.

However, it appears to be a balding man with hollow eye sockets, a nose, and lips. It is looking at me. The male face is completely three-dimensional, detailed, has different color shading, and there are no background features behind the image to create such a simulacra (false image) effect. The face appears against the darkened and far-away arched ceiling of the cell block. There are no surface structures on the plain concrete ceiling that could account for the man-like face in the photo.

The timing for the image's appearance is compelling evidence that it might represent a physical manifestation in the higher infrared range of light frequency. No one saw or heard anything unusual at the time, but Jack was getting a clairvoyant image of a man wanting us to come up to the gallery, and I loudly requested that he come down to us as we were not allowed up there.

Other Areas
Guard Tower:
Everyone was taken up the stairs and into the rooms leading to the prison guard tower. Nothing unusual occurred. The only interesting paranormal event for me

happened as I walked down the final stairs leading to a cell block below and the exit into the hub area. As I walked onto the landing and stepped down on the first stair, I smelled cigarette smoke. It was very strong but lasted only about ten seconds.

Renovated Cell Block 9:
This was an area being renovated for future public tours. It was well lighted in the front half, and all CCPRS and ECHO team members got a quick tour of the area.

Playing Field:
The outside playing field where prisoners played games or exercised, surrounded by the tall prison walls was not very active.

It's rumored that people see an apparition in the Guard Tower. Here is a shot showing an orb. *Photo by Katharine Sarro*

Out Buildings:

We were allowed to visit the dilapidated outbuildings near the hospital. No significant paranormal activity occurred anywhere. One particular room in the first building, however, intrigued me. It was some sort of maintenance room filled with large corroding equipment. The room had a peculiar triangular shape and was so full of machinery that I didn't want to enter it.

This room bothered me. I felt that something bad had happened in there and that someone was inside it. Later, I got a raspy EVP recording of a man saying, "Help me," just as I talk about the room to Jack and how the word, "trouble" came to mind when I looked into it.

Dowsing

At the end of the formal investigation, my original team returned to Cell Block 4 to do a dowsing session. This is a technique using metal dowsing rods to communicate with possible spirits. We asked *yes* and *no* questions which could be answered via the rods being manipulated by energies into the appropriate response positions.

Dowsing is a subjective technique, which may draw entities very close to us for further photography or other scientific documentation. As well as getting answers to our questions and possibly identifying entities, we are able to do historical research to validate our findings. The group decided that because there was high, anomalous EMF activity, I should dowse near the far rear cell, where the security guard saw an apparition and where we documented cold temperatures.

We may have made contact with two male entities during the dowsing session. The first male on the rods said he had lived in this cell block and possibly in a punishment cell. A second male took over very quickly and said that he was around forty years old and had lived on the cellblock.

Again, the males switched off, and the first male said that he had lived in the prison, but didn't die in his cell or inside the prison. He claimed to have died somewhere else on the prison property, but not in the hospital. He confirmed that he had been hurt by others who had caused his death, and had been sick and depressed before his death. He felt tied to the prison and afraid to move on because of what he'd done in life. However, he wanted to get out.

EVPs

EVPs (Electronic Voice Phenomena) are tape recordings of noises and voices that can't be accounted for in the environment at the time they were captured. They are more commonly called spirit voices or unexplained sounds that shouldn't be on the recording at all.

I recorded nineteen EVPs during the six-hour investigation of Eastern State Penitentiary. They are of various qualities. Some needed filtering with computer software and some were not completely clear, even with software enhancement. A brief list of them is below:

Cell Block 4:

1. Kyle asks: "Are you allowed to speak with us?" Unknown male response: "Hey! Hey!"

2. After the EVP session ends, an unknown male voice says, "Hey! Hey! Help me!"

3. As we walk out of the block, there is an unknown voice saying, "Perfect."

4. Another unknown response occurs. A male voice says, "I need to... myself."

Cell Block 12

5. Upon our entrance onto the second floor landing, I say, "It's cold." An unknown male voice says, "Hello."

6. During a quiet period, a very long and weird mechanical sound is heard.

7. The first time Mark's Walkie Talkie comes to life in the shower stall, the words, I ...help!" are heard coming from the radio.

8. Mark, Jack, and I are in the shower stall. I say, "It's really cold." Jack states (about the man he believes is in the corner), "He's really upset." As Jack makes his comment, a loud distressed male voice says, "Don't hit me again, please."

9. After Jack tells his story of seeing an orb, an unknown male whispers, "Jack."

Cell Block 9

While in the reconstructed cell block, I got several EVPs as the prison tour guide talked.

10. There is a male speaking in a whispering cadence. Sounds like he is speaking out numbers. Possibly prisoner numbers, which were used instead of names?

11. "I'm with you," male voice beside me.

12. "I want help," male voice beside me.

Outbuildings

13. As I stand in front of the triangular room, I recorded a whispering male cadence. Unclear EVP.

14. I am still in front of this room exclaiming that when I look into it, I get the word "trouble." A male response immediately after says, "Help me."

15. As Mark and I walk out of this same building, a male voice says, "Try to reach them."

Hub
(Center Area Where All Cell Block Ends Converge)

16. I recorded whispers and then a small child says, "I'm here." No children attended the investigation.

17. A child says angrily, "Come here, now!"

18. As Mark and I discuss our next plans, a child says, "I miss you."

Cell Block 4

19. During the dowsing there are intelligible whispers near me that do not come from team members.

Didn't I tell you it was chilling?! Be sure to visit the ECHO website to hear more about what this professional group is doing!

Tears in Cell Block 4

One of the CCPRS team members, Dinah, (mentioned in the ECHO report) had more to say about the incident of sadness on Cell Block 4. She says:

"This was the first time I'd ever experienced such a strong physical manifestation during a paranormal investigation. Cell Block 4 (the second cell from the end of the cell block on the left) gave me the most profound feeling of sadness I've ever felt. Having said that, I need to point out that the feelings were not connected to my own feelings in any way. It was as though an outside empathic sense took over my physical senses. Though I recognized the sadness, I could not feel it as mine. Tears came to my eyes and I had to fight a full-blown crying attack—that was so odd. Yet the tears were NOT mine—my body was only the conduit for the despair. I stayed in the area for several minutes, trying to understand the disconnect of my own feelings with the physical sensations that I could not control. I remember that the tour guide noted that this was the place she had seen a black male spirit in September 2006.

When Chris [from ECHO] began talking with the energy and asking what we could do for the spirit to help it, the word *Pray* kept popping into my mind, and I silently kept saying, *God Bless You*, over and over in my mind as the sadness gripped me.

Later, when we returned to the area for a dowsing exercise, I was somewhat hesitant to get close to the cell. I hung back from the others, watching from a distance. This was a strange feeling. It was as though a small safety switch inside me was warning me that I could be taken over again. Yet the feelings did not feel threatening in any way the first time to give me such pause. This second time, though, I had a mild aversion to sharing and feeling the sadness."

But still another interesting emotion was to grip two of my team members in both Cell Block 4 and Cell Block 12.

Dinah was having an internal battle with an unknown voice, as something in her mind kept whispering for her to find out if Kyle was all right. She kept hearing, "Is Kyle all right? Is Kyle all right?" And she was besieged with the thought, *must check on Kyle, must check on Kyle!* At first, she ignored it. Kyle, both a sensitive and professional investigator; he did not need a keeper! Still the thoughts intruded until she blurted out what she was hearing. It was then that Kyle advised that he was feeling as though he was being stabbed in his side. The pain made him double over.

The group stopped and circled him in a protective manner, as he talked about the feeling of being closed in by

The Teams investigate Cell Block 4 in the area where such sadness was felt. The orb on this photo shown at chest level of one of the team, is situated near this area of extreme sadness. This was also where it appeared that a shadow was moving from one cell to another. *Photo courtesy of Christine Gentry-Rodriguez*

an invisible force and stabbed. We discussed this and felt that an explanation might lie in that Kyle was an intimidating force due to his attire—camouflage pants, like military garb. It was possible that he was a threatening presence for the energy in the prison. He looked like an enforcer or guard.

Once we left Cell Block 12, Dinah no longer had those feelings of fear for Kyle.

Impressions of the Past

While visiting this decayed old prison, I kept imagining what it must have been like when it was first opened. It would have been clean, well kept—and its inhabitants would have been alive. In fact, Cell Block 12 was built in 1911, some seventy-one years after the prison was originally opened.

Interior Eastern State Penitentiary. *Photo by Katharine Sarro*

Now, the prison has trees literally growing in cell blocks, ceilings are dilapidated, and even pigeons make their presence known. The trees are actually referred to as "the urban jungle" by our guide through the prison. Look up, and you will see old catwalks in disrepair. If it's raining beware: you will be dripped on. On sunny days, look up and you will see a chipped ceiling. I keep musing to myself that this must have been beautiful when it was first built.

More Ghostly Occurrences

We found ourselves peeking into Death Row and, as I snapped some shots, we were shocked to hear the sound of whispering coming from the end of the hallway. This brought to mind an incident occurring on this cell block on a visit a few months prior to this investigation.

As a group, we'd decided to make a day trip to the prison. Upon approaching the area, it sounded as if someone was walking on the catwalk, but everything was gated, chained, and looking very decrepit.

We could hear the rain falling and dripping, but there was a distinct sound of footsteps coming from the above catwalk—where no one could get in or out. Asking one of the workers there, they advised that some areas are just too dangerous to go into because of the deteriorating conditions, and that Cell Block 14 was totally off limits at that time. So, there was *no chance* of someone playing a prank on us by walking above us.

On other occasions when I have visited the prison, during the daytime, I would be standing there still, with no wind blowing, yet it would be as if something was not only tugging on my shirt and my camera bag, but my braids

A bed left abandoned on Death Row. *Photo by Katharine Sarro*

as well. Quite often, out of the corner of my eye, I would think I saw a man wearing a dark uniform standing at the end of one of the corridors.

There are accounts that prison guards still watch from the rotunda and from the guard towers. Apparently, a figure of a man has been seen high in a guard tower that is now inaccessible due to crumbling and broken stairs. It is here, where I got a most interesting photograph. In this photo, there is an incredibly bright light called an orb, which is a round object that appears and emits its own light.

The odd thing was, it is truly impossible for anyone to be up in this guard tower, because there are no stairs leading up to it! The stairs have all crumbled and fallen apart.

Orbs in general have been showing up in a lot of photos because of the advent of the digital camera. Many times, an orb is the pixelization that happens when using a camera with low mega-pixels. Essentially, as the digital camera takes the photo, it then fills in some areas. (This shot is taken with my new Canon EOS Digital Rebel XT camera with 8 mega-pixels.)

During investigations, we use several devices to record the changes in the atmosphere, an EMF detector measures the electromagnetic currents in the atmosphere. During a previous preliminary investigation, an EMF reading of 3 up to 5 was found all along the wall surrounding the prison. (See the Glossary for a more in depth look at equipment usages and the meanings of readings.)

According to historical accounts, things were smuggled into the inmates by throwing things over the wall. In fact, during ball games, balls were purposefully hit over the wall and returned with contraband such as cigarettes and even money hidden within the balls.

I am informed that there is even the ghost of a dog which inhabits the prison. Apparently, in 1924, a dog named Pep was sentenced as "the cat murdering dog." Pep was assigned inmate number C2559 and served a life sentence for murdering the Governor's wife's cherished cat. One of the shadows glimpsed on occasion is close to the floor, and has a quick step, that sounds like an animals claws hitting the floor…so perhaps it is "Pep."

During restoration in Cell Block 4, there is an incredible account in which a locksmith was working on removing a 140-year-old lock from a cell door when an amazingly powerful force overcame him so strongly that he was unable to move. Some say that when he removed the key, it opened a portal or a gateway to the horrifyingly chilling past events which occurred at Eastern State—and that action offered the spirits trapped within the Penitentiary a way out.

"Entry Hallway, 1992": From *Hope Abandoned: Eastern State Penitentiary* by Mark Perrott, 1999.

In the locksmith's account he speaks of "an out-of-body experience" as he was sucked into a negative energy which seemed to bust right out of the cell. Distorted forms swirled around, anguished faces seemed to appear on the cell's walls, and an unusual form beckoned him. The man still shudders in fear to this day when he recalls his vivid and terrifying experience.

Both employees and tourists have reported hearing whispering, giggling, and even weeping coming from within the walls of the prison. Employees have mentioned seeing "The Soap Lady" which is said to reside in the last cell on the second floor and is clothed in white. It was on the second floor that the women of the prison were housed.

The bottom ghostly line is that not only is Eastern State Penitentiary a prison that is infamous in historic content, it is also haunted by that same theme. Its ghosts continue to keep alive a tradition of passing on, from one life to the next, the eerie channel of events long since gone and the ever moving passing of time forgotten. Visit, if you dare. You won't be disappointed.

Chapter Two
Ghostly Haunts Around Town

Independence Hall

Independence Hall, located on Third and Chestnut Street, not only houses the constitution, but there is believed to be a ghostly specter haunting the clock tower, and an apparition is seen clothed in eighteenth-century garb.

Perhaps our forefathers are traversing the halls along with those who are brave enough to be security guards at this noted landmark. Just imagine hearing footsteps from above, when you know no one is upstairs, and all of a sudden, right in front of your eyes, a smoky apparition appears seemingly out of nowhere!

The City Tavern

The City Tavern is located in the Society Hill-Old City area of Philadelphia, located at Second and Walnut Streets. It is a place where George Washington, Ben Franklin, and Thomas Jefferson were amongst some of the Tavern's most famous diners! Although nowadays, I'm sure that even some cool movie stars and rock and rollers like to check this place out, too.

It's an amazing place to eat because not only is the food fantastic, but there are a few interesting ghost stories as well. In the City Tavern, a former waiter apparently continues to work. A bar room duel ended in the death

Independence Hall. *Photo by Katharine Sarro*

of a man who still likes to adjust the table settings so the silverware clinks and moves when no one is around. A man in a white is shirt is sometimes seen spotted with blood, and falling to the floor, and then he mysteriously disappears.

There is also the ghost of a young woman seen wearing a bridal dress and veil. In the original tavern, a young woman waiting for her betrothed was killed in a fire. It seems that in the 1800s, a young woman was enjoying her bridal party, when suddenly, one of the sconces caught fire on one of the curtains billowing in the breeze, and set the upstairs of the tavern aflame. So now, she has been said to mysteriously make her presence known during bridal parties by showing up as a specter in photographs, draining the batteries of cameras, and even causing some patrons to feel a burning hand upon them.

Betsy Ross House

Located at 239 Arch Street, this historic landmark is quite haunted. Betsy is known for being the seamstress of the first American flag and rented this property, along with her husband, between 1773 and 1786.

The seamstress is said to be seen haunting her home, where she is reported to be witnessed crying at the foot of a bed. She is also seen at her burial site there. (She has also been buried at varied times at South 5th Street near Locust, Mount Moriah Cemetery—you'll hear about this place later on!—as well as Arch Street in the courtyard near the Betsy Ross House.

Carpenter's Historic Hall

Carpenter's Historic Hall, located on 3rd and Chestnut Streets in Philadelphia, has reported that the former inhabitants of the apartments, and even members of the 1774 First Continental Congress, haunt the building. Reports include ghostly apparitions of its former tenants wandering the halls and the sound of footsteps walking around. There are accounts that the hall is haunted by the nations first group of bank robbers, who, in 1798, knocked off a city bank.

Cresheim Cottage

Cresheim Cottage, located on Germantown Avenue in the Mount Airey section of Philadelphia, was originally built in 1748. There are reports that a young girl, which has been named "Emily" by the owners, wearing a pink Victorian-style dress with beautiful dark locks in corkscrew curls, has been witnessed running around the location. Mysteriously, an attic door will open and close, and odd unexplainable thumps were heard in the hallways during renovations. (It is well known in ghost circles that renovations tend to stir up spirits!)

The Civil War Library and Museum

The Spirits of Soldiers have been witnessed playing a game of cards in The Lincoln Room in The Civil War Library and Museum. Apparently the soldiers' spirits are so intent upon their game that they remain unaware that they are being watched as they play long into the evening hour.

The Crier in the Country

The ghostly inhabitants of The Crier in The Country Restaurant continue to party after hours even after the restaurant is closed and the hall is empty. A third floor bedroom, a ladies room and even the Lydia Room are all areas that activity is encountered.

Psychic and investigator Laurie Hull, founder of Delaware County Paranormal Research says when asked about her experiences in the book, *Brandywine Ghosts*:

"We were unable to make contact with the spirit of Lydia, but we did experience the nasty spirit on the third floor. As I entered the bedroom with two other psychics, I was flooded with images of a young girl, cowering on her bed, which was in the corner. A very large man was advancing towards her. The vision became too much for me, so I had to leave the room."

So beware when entering the bathrooms or seeking company on the third floor, you may feel like you are being watched…or worse.

Camac Street Ghost

A friend reported to me in confidence a strange ghostly experience on Camac Street:

"One night, in early spring, sometime around 1990 or 1991, it was a warm night, so I was joyriding on my BMX bike around center city… It had just rained that day and the streets were still wet; I was sober and in a clear state of mind, and I was riding down Pine Street, and turned onto Camac Street going north to get to Spruce Street. Towards the middle of Camac, I saw an older white gentleman walking towards me, (south) and he looked pale, and as if he might be sleep walking. He was dressed in dark pajamas, a white t-shirt, and a loose cotton robe.

"I said to myself, *That's odd; I hope that dude is not senile and wandering around*... I was not interested in a confrontation with a 'weirdo,' so I left him behind. Two seconds later, I am a bit further up the street and I felt a strong urge to look behind me again—just to see of the dude was all right. ...And the sidewalk was empty; no one was on that street but me. I heard no door opening or shutting, or any car door opening or shutting, or ignition starting—no possible way for that dude to disappear!

"I was spooked, and I kept riding on ... But I thought to myself, *That guy looked like a ghost, like someone confused and lost.* So, to this day, I call that my ultimate ghost story—one second he was on the sidewalk, and the next second he was gone!"

The Inn Philadelphia

The Inn Philadelphia is located at 251 South Camac on one of the oldest blocks in the city. And it has a playful ghost that enjoys pulling on the hair of its clientele. Pictures will mysteriously fly off of the walls, the brass chandeliers sway for no reason at all, and noisy footsteps are heard in the upstairs dining room.

When I was personally there, the chandeliers were swaying to and fro, and I thought I saw a man standing in the doorway. I remember asking why he was dressed in costume—if there was an actor around getting ready for a tour of *Philly*. Since there are ghost tours about, that's what I thought he was going to do. Apparently, though, no one else saw who I was talking about!

The Academy of Music

The Academy of Music, built in 1857 and located on the Avenue of the Arts at Broad and Locust, is a grand building with an amazing history. It is the oldest Opera

House in the United States that is still currently in use. The Academy of Music is the home of the Opera Company of Philadelphia, and hosts the Pennsylvania Ballet, and a series of national Broadway productions—"Broadway at the Academy." Since 1900, the Academy of Music had been the home of the Philadelphia Orchestra, which has since moved its home base to the Kimmel Center. The Philadelphia Orchestra continues to return every year in January to play the Academy of Music Concert and Ball.

Some historical and notable patrons and performers are: President Ulysses S. Grant, John Phillip Sousa (first introduced "Stars and Stripes Forever"), Martha Graham (performed in Igor Stravinsky's "The Rite of Spring"), Marian Anderson, Maria Callas, and Enrico Caruso. These are just a few who have amazed opera goers. President Grover Cleveland, along with his newlywed wife, attended

The Academy of Music, located on the corner of Broad and Locust, on the Avenue of the Arts. *Photo by Katharine Sarro*

a gala celebration of the Centennial U.S. Constitution in 1886. There is a room dedicated to Eugene Ormandy— President Richard Nixon presented Eugene Ormandy with the Presidential Medal of Freedom in 1970.

Maureen Lynch, who has been working at The Academy of Music for twenty years, now responded to my question, "Do you think the Academy of Music has any ghosts?"

"I strongly sense there are *angels* that watch over the building. So many times, I, and other staff, find ourselves going to a location in the building, that was not our original destination—for no reason—only to discover why we should be there …discovering something, however minor, that is always in the best interest of the building.

"Were we led there? I feel a very spiritual essence whenever I am in the building. There is a warmth and comfort here that we all 'understand' but don't discuss. We translate it as 'we love the Academy and we love working here.'

"My personal feeling is that comfort comes from the angels who watch over the building here at the Academy of Music. My theory is that they are the many artists who have graced our stage, but no longer walk among us. Why wouldn't they protect the places where their art came alive? Also, among the angels, would be many patrons who loved coming to the Academy and our civic and institutional leaders who nourished her history. I doubt our commitments end with this lifetime's reality.

"I often stand on the empty stage at night when the building is empty, and just look up at the balconies. Amid that silence, with just the bare bulb on a stand, the traditional *ghost light* positioned in the middle of the stage, I contemplate all that has happened in the world since 'she' was built, before the Civil War…and I am amazed that 'The Grand Old Lady' continues to thrive so beautifully.

"For me, the Academy is magical and inspiring—a spiritual space even. …Guess which building I will watch over if the next reality allows us that option?!"

An anonymous source told me that she was wandering in the area below the stage when someone tapped her on the shoulder. She spun around to see who was there, but no one was in sight. She happened to see some lights flickering as if there was a light about to go out. Once backstage, she said she mentioned it to someone and they said that they would look into it. Perhaps the tap on the shoulder was all the spirit needed to make sure that people walking in the "catacombs" of the Academy of Music would not be left in the dark.

"The interesting thing is my batteries go dead all the time." (I've heard this from a few people who work within the Academy's walls.) "As far as 'the empty seat' story, I don't know about that one.....it's a bit of a rumor." Chills in the wings; who could it be standing by, waiting before making a grand entrance? Perhaps the great Caruso or Maria Callas linger in the wings watching performances…

Even the operas have ghosts! Gaetano Donezetti's Lucia *di Lammermoor*, one of the leading bel canto operas, is based on the novel by Sir Walter Scott, *The Bride of Lammermoor*. In Lucia's famous aria, "Regnava nel Silenzio," Lucia tells her maid that she has just seen the ghost of a girl. The opera *Macbeth*, Giuseppe Verdi, in the famous banquet scene, Macbeth sees the ghost of Banquo and goes into a rage. His terrified guests leave thinking that Macbeth has gone mad.

The Walnut Street Theater

The Walnut Street Theater, a historic Philadelphia institution located at 825 Walnut Street at the corner of 9th and Walnut, was founded in 1809, and is boasted as being *America's Oldest Theatre*. But that's not the only old thing about this national landmark! It's been reported that there is an apparition of a little girl from the 1900s. There's also a few ghostly patrons of the theater who return and expect to sit in their usual seats. Theatergoers have reported to have heard unanticipated "voices" that have shocked people literally out of their seats. An anonymous source told me that she was sitting with a friend, when an elderly couple asked them why they were in their seats. She and her date looked again at their tickets, and they were, in fact, seated correctly. As they turned to look back at the older couple, the two elderly patrons had simply vanished.

Orleans 8

A little girl haunts the Orleans 8 Movie Theater projection room. Late in the evening, the little girl can be heard asking people to play with her and giggles a lot. Maybe the theater will have to add to their shushing of people during a film to include quieting a ghost…

City Hall

City Hall is located on what was once a public gallows. There were many horrid cases, but one seems to stand out the most—the case of a Native American, Joseph Hightower. He was believed to have murdered a Quaker family and was found guilty and executed on the gallows. Joseph Hightower maintained his innocence to the bitter end and proclaimed that he would "avenge himself…" Shortly after Hightower's death, the arresting officer drowned and the attorney for the prosecution was run over by a carriage. There are reports of a swinging and swaying "dark shadow" in the courtyard with spectral feet dangling at eye level.

Allen's Lane

Witnesses say that late at night on Allen's Lane there is an apparition of a soldier wearing revolutionary clothing. The scary part is that he is seen carrying his severed head.

The Drake Tower

This former luxury hotel, built in 1929, has now been converted into apartments. The top six floors are home to sixteen penthouses with beautiful spacious terraces. There have been accounts of people witnessing parties occurring, not in our present-day surroundings, but in the late twenties and early thirties. It's as if there is a window looking into another time, seeing a parallel universe.

Merchants Exchange

Merchants Exchange is located on 3rd and Walnut. There has been an apparition seen standing on the portico described as a man dressed in nineteenth-century clothing. He appears late in the evening until dawn and quickly disappears when the sound of phantom hoof beats are heard.

History accounts a tale of a beggar named Jack Osteen who would frequently station himself at Merchant's Exchange. Jack was known to be a great entertainer who loved to sing and tell stories, and would wait for a rich man to hire him. While waiting, Jack would often pat and feed the horses, and one horse in particular became very fond of Jack. Harold Thorn was the owner of the beloved horse. Fortunately enough, the horse did not take after its owner, Howard Thorn.

Harold Thorn was known to be an unscrupulous, greedy, and condescending man. One day, Mr. Thorn lost a lot of money in a bad business deal and came bursting outside. Mr. Jack Osteen, who was blind, mistakenly stepped on Mr. Thorn's foot. In a rage, Thorn furiously beat Mr. Osteen to death with his walking stick.

Thorn's horse then reared, shrieked and wailed, and pummeled Mr. Thorn to death. It is said that the specters seen here are in fact, Mr. Osteen and Mr. Thorn, and the sound of the hoof beats belong to Mr. Thorn's horse. Perhaps the spirits are caught in a residual haunting—a kind of loop playing over and over again. The same apparitions appear at the same time in a sequential manner, much like what is described in this story.

As an investigator, I get asked numerous questions regarding hauntings and how to deal with them. I always tell people to start a journal. Make a note of what is happening: what time, where, what exactly is happening, how long it lasts—note every single detail. This often helps determine what kind of haunting is occurring. The difference between a residual and an intelligent haunting is this: With an intelligent haunting, one actually interacts with the spirit. In a residual haunting, a scene plays out despite those watching and without spirit/human interaction. In the case of the Merchant's Exchange, the ghostly forms do not interact with watchers, but rather move through their own scene regardless of what goes on about them.

Washington Square Park

A strange tale occuring at Washington Square Park was told to me by a woman, who prefers to remain anonymous:

"One day, I was walking home from work on my way through Washington Square Park, when a gentleman approached me and asked me if I wanted him to sing for me. With no time for me to respond, he dropped to his knees and sang in a beautiful tenor voice 'Vesti La Giubba' from 'Pagliacci.' I looked around to see other people's reactions, but no one was around. He was dressed in an old tattered nineteenth-century cloak. In that second when I turned to look for someone else's reaction to this gentleman and realizing no one else was around, I turned back and he had disappeared. I was just flabbergasted! Had I just witnessed a ghost?"

(This report fits the definition of an intelligent haunting. In this case, a woman was actually interacting with a spirit.)

The memorial to the unknown soldier where the flame always remains lit in Washington Square Park. *Photo by Katharine Sarro*

There are a few specters lurking in Washington Square Park besides our singing romantic. The ghost of Leah is seen; she is hunched over and swaddled in a dark blanket. A few people have reported seeing her as a woman cloaked in a long, dark blanket that seemed to be very out of place in the park. "I saw this old woman," an anonymous person began. "She was all bent over, and she looked sick. I wanted to help her. I walked over to her, but she just vanished…I thought I was losing it."

The Unknown Soldier's epitaph reads, "Liberty is a light for which many men have died in darkness." Washington Square Park, the original Memorial to the "unknown soldier," is the burial ground for about two thousand bodies, which include American and British Revolutionary War Soldiers. It is here that one will see "shadows."

There used to be a prison located across the street that was occupied by the British during the war. Most unfortunately, hundreds of prisoners where treated cruelly and died, and their bodies were buried here along with numerous British and Hessian soldiers, and even the bodies of those who perished from "yellow fever." It's no wonder they remain in an unrest state. They are the shadows of our past, come back to…

The Powel House

In the 200 block of South 3rd Street is The Powel House, where Samuel and Elizabeth Powel invited notable guests such as Washington, Lafayette, Franklin, and *anybody who was anybody* in Colonial Philadelphia. This historic home is not only a private residence, but also houses a few spirits. There has been a sighting of a young woman who was described to have been fanning herself and tapping her foot, and even the spirit of an officer sporting a blue uniform has been seen—-perhaps the spirit of Marquis de Lafayette…

Franklin Square Park

Located at 4th and Race Streets in a portion of Franklin Square Park, this park was one of William Penn's original five squares. It has been refurbished and there is now a carousel, a lovely fountain, and even a miniature golf course. There is an old subterranean station that lies beneath Franklin Square Park which was built in 1936, and was last used in 1979. Oh, and it is also the place where the ghost of a young woman has been seen…

Water Street

Amongst the ghost stories, I found some peculiar pirate tales, one of which concerns Water Street. This area was, for many years, the stomping ground of vagabond pirates who would march up and down Walnut and Front Streets. A Scottish Pirate, Wilkinson, had murdered a man in Marcus Hook and had killed three others in Wilmington. He was finally captured and taken into custody. During his capture, a dozen of his men were killed. Wilkinson was finally hanged after an attempted escape from the Walnut Street Prison.

Apparently, an apparition of a pirate has been spotted walking down Water Street. An anonymous source told me, "I thought this dude was dressed up for some party; I wanted to get a look at his outfit and his sword, cause it looked pretty cool. But as I got closer, he turned the corner and just vanished. I was pretty creeped out!" And I can see why!

The Moshulu

Lanterns sit atop the tables located in the Moshulu, and rumor has it that they have some extra help in keeping them lit. The lanterns are blown out every night before close, and yet some of them relight with a little ghostly assistance. Even in the daylight the lanterns mysteriously light. The workers check and recheck the lanterns periodically, and continuously have to blow them out in the daytime!

Guests and workers have heard footsteps and quiet voices which almost seem as if they come from the rigging of the ship. Even the laughing of a woman can be heard after hours.

As I sat having dinner with a friend, who happens to be a psychic, I was astonished at what she was telling me. She said, "It's not coming from the rigging…" I looked at her quizzically, and she got up and proceeded to wander around. When she returned, she quietly said, "I never imagined how many lives were lost on this ship; now I know the truth!"

She went on to say that "a woman has lost her life here… something very strange and deceitful happened." Then she went on to say, "Please enjoy your dinner; I have an odd feeling this may be your last time enjoying this type of food." Sure enough, I've developed a seafood allergy, much to my dismay, because that lobster was delicious! Someone from beyond knew before I did…

The Rodin Museum

The Rodin Museum is located on Benjamin Franklin Parkway and has a beautiful garden with benches that couples will find themselves cuddling amongst—yup—

ghosts. You see, there is a sad love story about a sweet couple who used to meet often in the garden of the Rodin Museum. The young lady was Rachel, the daughter of a prominent Rittenhouse family. The young man, Hank, was from Brewerytown, from the "other side of the tracks," so to speak. Their love of sculpture, art, and the beautiful garden brought the two lovers together.

Rachel's father, furious that she was dating someone of a low social status, sent Rachel away to a boarding school in upstate New York. When she finally returned to Philadelphia, she went to the Museum's garden to find Hank. She did not find him there; she went to his home only to find it boarded up. Desperate to find Hank, she asked around and found out that Hank was sent to Vietnam and that his mother had passed away.

Grief stricken, she walked back to the garden and suddenly turned and dashed into the busy parkway where she was struck by an oncoming automobile. She was killed immediately in front of her favorite garden. Locals and tourists have seen a loving couple cuddling, that simply seems to vanish.

The Waterworks

Behind the Art Museum of Philadelphia stands the Waterworks, which is a beautiful building located on the banks of the Schuylkill River. A rotunda overlooks the river where one can view Boathouse Row and have a pretty view of the museum. It is here that two very famous ghosts like to roam: One is Benjamin Franklin and the other is literary genius Edgar Allen Poe. Poe was intimately involved with his writing—as well as his decline and disheartenment towards life—while living in

The Rodin Museum has a sweet yet sad ghost story about lost love. *Photo by Katharine Sarro*

The Waterworks is located behind the Art Museum. A beautiful place to stroll along and perhaps catch a glimpse of the ghost of Benjamin Franklin or even Edgar Allen Poe. *Photo by Katharine Sarro*

Philadelphia. And this was one of Benjamin Franklin's favorite places. Is Poe here at the Waterworks still mourning his young wife's death while Franklin just spends quality time?

North Philadelphia

In North Philadelphia, on Germantown Avenue and Cecil B. Moore Avenue, there used to be a Methodist Church where a young woman named Clara was laid to rest in a vault under the floor of the old house of worship. It is here on this corner that an apparition of a young woman wearing a wedding dress appears. She is disheveled and sobbing for her love, James, to return.

The story is a sad one: Clara was waiting for her beloved groom to appear for their wedding; however, he never arrived for the ceremony. In fact, he had jilted her for someone else, and actually left the state of Pennsylvania. Clara was consumed with grief and would call out for him constantly; nothing and no one was able to console her. She withered away in sadness and finally passed away.

The church has since been turned into a social hall in the late nineteenth century. People who continue to attend this social hall say they have seen this sad girl in a disheveled wedding dress…waiting…

Osol Hall, University of the Sciences

Osol Hall was originally a psychiatric institute. Legend has it that a young girl who was admitted there went crazy due to being mistreated. She committed suicide on the sixth floor. A few years later, the institute was turned into dormitory and apartment suites for the students of the University of Sciences, Philadelphia.

Residents have reported hearing strange noises; bathroom doors which were closed are seen propped open. In the men's bathroom, a bizarre moment for the guys is when the toilet lids they are sure have been left up, are suddenly closed. Residents have also mentioned an eerie feeling of being watched, and get all sorts of bizarre sensations and feelings that they just don't quite understand.

Philadelphia University—Textiles

The University was once a small Catholic school for girls. A nun was reported to have hung herself after finding out that she had been impregnated by the father. She hung herself in the top room of the mansion where the attic is located. Though the attic remains locked, an image of a nun is seen standing near the window of the top floor.

The old classrooms have now been converted into a dormitory where incidences including odd noises, such as footsteps, are heard, and bright white glowing balls keep appearing in pictures.

Apparently, if one sits on the hill in front of the mansion, the apparition of the nun can be witnessed around sunrise.

The Institute of Pennsylvania

The elevators at the Institute of Pennsylvania open with a loud resounding noise, and often voices and footsteps are heard coming out of the elevators—when there are no people.

Saint Mary's Annex at Saint Joseph's University

Located on the outskirts of Saint Joseph's campus, this old converted convent has quite a few ghostly inhabitants, most of which are nuns who are seen walking in the hallways. Reports of footsteps and laughter are heard along with other "odd bumps in the night."

Original Chapel of The Saint Andrews Church

The older chapel is located next to the newer church. The original chapel is now an annex. Reports of hazy white figures have been seen in and around the area and odd noises have been heard, coming from the woods behind the buildings.

Saint Dominic's Catholic School

There are reports of a ghostly specter seen in the graveyard.

Bright Hope Baptist Church

After a majority of the parishioners have departed from the church, there are "sounds of unsettlement" which can be heard coming from the back of the building.

Chapter Three
Edgar Allen Poe

Edgar Allen Poe was born in Boston, Massachusetts, on January 19, 1809. He is considered by many to be "the father of the modern mystery." Poe was educated in Virginia and England as a child. It was in his later years at West Point that Poe began to show an incredible propensity for writing prose. At the age of fifteen, he wrote these words in memory of a female acquaintance, "The requiem for the loveliest dead that ever died so young."

Poe was to work for a few publications as both editor and contributor. His career as an editor coincided with his growth as an author. While Poe worked in Philadelphia for Burton's "Gentleman's Magazine" in 1839, his work continued to grow and flourish. It was at this time in his career that he still was financially insecure; however, his work was being recognized and praised. This helped greatly in furthering his reputation.

During his tenure at Burton's, he wrote the macabre tales: "The Fall of the House of Usher," and "William Wilson." These psychological thrillers were to become Poe's trademark. In 1841, Poe began working for George Graham. Graham offered Edgar Allen Poe $800 a year to work for him as an editor. While working for Graham, Poe began to prepare his famous work, "The Murders in the Rue Morgue," for publication. The story was published in April 1841, and featured Auguste C. Dupin, the first-ever fictional detective.

The raven is mounted on Edgar Allen Poe's haunted home here in Philadelphia.
Photo by Katharine Sarro

During these years in Philadelphia, Poe published his trademark horror tales, "The Tell-Tale Heart," and "The Pit and The Pendulum." In 1845, Poe's famous poem, "The Raven," was published and he finally achieved his true rise to fame. The public's reaction to the poem brought Poe true recognition.

Edgar Allen Poe once resided at 7th and Spring Garden, in Philadelphia, however, it is uncertain about how long he actually lived at this address. Any furnishings which may have belonged to the family have simply vanished, and now the house remains empty. As one walks through the now vacant house, the floors groan and squeak at every step.

Edgar Allen Poe wrote, in addition to the work noted prior, "The Black Cat," "The Gold-Bug," "The Masque of the Red Death," "The Purloined Letter," "The Cask of Amontillado," "A Descent into the Maelstrom," "The Man of the Crowd," "The Oval Portrait," and apparently, he began writing "The Raven" while living in the house on North 7th Street. He had another residence in Philadelphia located at 2502 Fairmount Avenue. At both residences, he lived with his wife, Virginia, and his mother-in-law.

In January of 1842, Poe's wife, Virginia Clemm, ruptured a blood vessel; she recovered partially, however, her health would steadily decline. Her last five years were a weary cycle of recuperation and relapse, and unfortunately, Poe's mental health seemed to mirror Virginia's cycle of recovery and decline. In February of 1847, Virginia ultimately died of consumption.

Poe was thoroughly distraught by his young wife's death and he wrote, "Deep in earth my love is lying and I must weep alone." Poe's downward cycle began when his lovely wife died. He suffered and survived a suicide attempt; he had a horrible ordeal with alcoholism and severe depression. Poe died a tragic death in October of 1849, in Baltimore, Maryland. It is said that the circumstances behind his death remain unknown; however, it appears that it was his addiction to alcohol which may have ultimately caused his death.

Poe's ghost is said to be seen walking behind The Waterworks, and apparently also haunts the General Wayne Inn in Malvern, Pennsylvania. Those who see him, find him sitting near a window writing. It remains a mystery whether his ghost haunts the house on 7th Street. Listen to the floorboards as they creek and maybe you will hear a tale whispered from beyond the grave of Edgar Allen Poe himself.

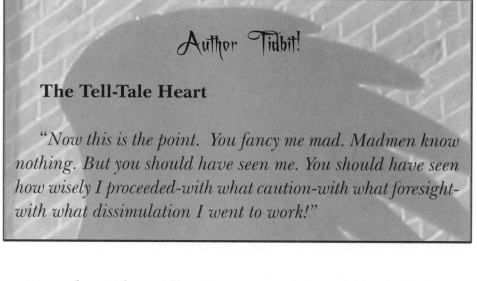

Author Tidbit!

The Tell-Tale Heart

"Now this is the point. You fancy me mad. Madmen know nothing. But you should have seen me. You should have seen how wisely I proceeded-with what caution-with what foresight-with what dissimulation I went to work!"

Just what Edgar Allen Poe was writing while sitting near that window at The General Wayne Inn? This will forever remain a mystery, for only Poe himself knows.

Chapter Four
Specters Lurking in the Outskirts

Just a hop, skip, and a jump from Philadelphia—and definitely worth a trip—are some ghostly haunts that are worth your time to "see!"

The General Wayne Inn

Even the outskirts of Philadelphia have intriguing specters that should be noted. In Malvern, Pennsylvania, are two such haunted locations: The General Wayne Inn and Penn Rynn Manor.

The General Wayne Inn is renowned for having the ghost of Edgar Allen Poe, who is often seen writing by the window. But Poe is not the only spectral haunt at this famous inn. It's also reportedly haunted by the ghosts of two Hessian soldiers, two women, an African American male, and a Native American Indian.

Outside The General Wayne Inn, the specter of a young soldier has been seen walking amongst the tombstones of a nearby cemetery.

Penn Rynn

The old Penn Rynn Manor is located right on the Delaware River and used to be the Biddle Estate. According to legend, one of the sons of the original owners had fallen in love with a servant. Because the love was forbidden, due to their social differences, they slipped away to the river together, where they disappeared into the water as one and never returned. There are accounts of the lovers' apparitions appearing as a young woman riding a white horse and a young man who walks up and down the path from the house to the riverbank.

The Rusty Nail

While out on the town, beware of the ghouls who roam freely in the streets—and even in the nightclubs and bars. The Rusty Nail, located in Lehighton, invites you to celebrate with such a tale. Apparently, one of the owners of the Rusty Nail committed suicide and still, to this day, resides at the bar by an old leather-covered cabinet door.

It just so happens that I am friendly with some band members who play music at the Rusty Nail. When I was there, I did not see any ghosts so to speak, but I remember one of the guys getting spooked while sitting at the bar. We were relaxing and having drinks, when he thought someone had tapped him on the shoulder and blamed *me* for it. I had not, so I laughed and he just sat there and looked a little freaked out. (I'm glad that I'm not the only one plagued by ghostly tricks!)

Byberry Mental Hospital

Byberry Mental Hospital was established in the early 1900s and was abandoned in the early 90s due to poor living conditions, the reportedly atrocious mistreatment of its patients, and because some of the buildings contained asbestos. People who have intrepidly snuck into the catacombs report seeing no living things whatsoever.

For example, all the birds on the ground were dead, the maggots next to the birds, dead. Kind of gross, but unfortunately true! It seems that some of those who have been brave enough to steal into this condemned area have only run back out screaming and crying. Those who are a little more adventurous have found interesting artifacts, such as old patients' reels, scalpels, bottles, and former patients' artwork—it's all creepy stuff.

Now federal property, some buildings have been torn down. There have been rumors that apparitions have frightened people into running scared out of its underground catacombs. Those that I know who have been bold enough to check this place out, have told me that, although they saw no ghosts, they had the creepy feeling that they were being watched. I was told that all the murals on the walls, along with the empty medicine bottles and regalia left behind, gave the place a distinctive and bizarre atmosphere.

Some have reported that they are so haunted by the memories of what they saw at Byberry that they will never be the same again.

(Please note that this area may be illegal to trespass upon. Follow the rules so you don't get into trouble!)

Friends Hospital

Friends Hospital, which was built in the early 1800s, has a few ghostly reports of doors opening and closing when no one is around, and a female seen walking in the hallways who resembles the wife of a former superintendent. Those that work there have said that often they get the feeling that they are being watched and that they get a bit creeped out when the doors open and close on their own. In fact, when I had to go to Friends Hospital years ago, I was told that I bore a bit of a resemblance to a ghostly apparition seen there. Now that *really* freaked me out!

Chapter Five
Fort Mifflin

Exterior shot of the General's barracks at Fort Mifflin. *Photo by Katharine Sarro*

Fort Mifflin, the only Revolutionary War Battlefield which is still intact, is located only a few minutes from downtown; it is so close to the airport that as you arrive you can actually see it from the plane. It was originally built in 1771, and used by the U.S. Army until 1952.

General George Washington ordered the garrison at Fort Mifflin to hold off the British Navy, in order for the Continental Army to make its way to the Valley Forge encampment safely during the Revolutionary War. According to General Washington, the Delaware River was "of the utmost importance to America."

Named after Commandant Thomas Mifflin, this fort is most likely one of the most haunted places in the United States. There are numerous stories and accounts of the ghostly apparitions that are meandering about throughout the buildings and casemates of Fort Mifflin. Moorestown Ghost Research has gone back on several occaisions; so have members of our group, Chester County Paranormal Research Society. Rodney Anonymous, songwriter and vocalist of the famous punk band "The Dead Milkmen," did his best to spend a night in casemate five. Go check out his experiences online called, "A Bad Night at Fort Mifflin" (http://www.rodneyanonymous.com/radio/mifflin.html).

Apparently Rodney heard "popping" sounds and originally thought it was Wayne. His cell phone battery dies, and the recorder left alone on a window sill, mysteriously flips itself over. This gives pause for thought—if a tough guy in one of my favorite punk bands gets creeped out by Fort Mifflin, then I don't feel so bad at all.

Fort Mifflin is an intriguing and fascinating tourist attraction. Occasionally, there are reenactments, complete with cannons fired and soldiers dressed in uniform. There are even special events known as "Sleeping with the Ghosts" that are held during the warmer seasons—otherwise you might shiver and freeze in the casemates.

Fort Mifflin is one of famous paranormal investigator John Zaffis's favorite spots to do investigations, and is quickly gaining popularity not only from tourists, but also from avid paranormal researchers. Fort Mifflin is now by far one of my favorite spots, so is Eastern State Penitentiary, but Fort Mifflin has a very different aura and feeling. Its easy to get swept away by looking at the beautiful landscape at Fort Mifflin, and gazing at fourteen of their restored buildings, but watch out; you may just see one of their many ghosts lurking amongst the casemates, General's quarters, and the magazines.

An Earlier Visit

The first time I ever went to Fort Mifflin was about ten years ago. My boyfriend at the time thought it would be fun. I thought it sounded cool, too, so we found ourselves wandering around this historic masterpiece and checking everything out.

I was bewildered to keep seeing this adorable little girl in an old-fashioned dress with these beautiful ribbons. I told her to be careful on the hill. There was a sign there that warned visitors to stay off the magazines, and I wanted her to tell me where her parents were so I could help her. She just smiled and giggled and tossed her curly, blonde hair.

I said to my boyfriend that I was concerned that this girl's parents weren't paying attention to her. My boyfriend kept looking around and replied, "I don't know what you're talking about. I don't see the girl you're describing!" I stammered and pointed; he grabbed my hand, and we left immediately. Much to my frustration and dismay, I was not able to find her parents. He was not able to see the girl—much less the parents.

So, ten years later, I have returned, and I am not so shocked when I start to learn the history of Fort Mifflin's spirits. There are accounts of a little girl's ghost.

New and Improved

This time no one is going to grab my hand and make me leave. If anything, I will grab someone's hand and run *towards* any apparition I see. As we head back to Casemate Five, I feel slight trepidation. Once situated,

Interior of Casemate 5 in Fort Mifflin. *Photo by Katharine Sarro*

I feel incredibly overwhelmed. I have been informed by good sources of spiritual "Holiness" (as I shall refer to them) that I am an intuitive, clairaudient, and clairvoyant amongst a few of the oddball abilities I have. This is what makes me the slightly quirky person I am—one who is quite often incredibly misunderstood. So the feelings are strong here. As I sit down, I feel as if someone is leaning against my legs.

My team settles in and we begin some EVP work. I was stunned by the EVPs we got from a preliminary investigation, and I am excited by what I am sensing now. Visions start flooding my mind and I feel like the room is spinning. There is a man who is bloody from head to toe; I can barely make out his face, and his head seems disjointed from his body. The other men have lines of blood drawn on them and moan in agony. Not a pleasant experience, but nonetheless, I remain quiet and intrigued. EVPs have proven to be amazing and have corroborated what I have sensed.

There are sounds of gunfire and moans. A man's voice says, "I just want to go to the chair." Another EVP reveals a man's voice saying, "Come back."

On a previous occasion, some of our teammates had visited Fort Mifflin and had an odd experience here. They were hanging out in Casemate Five, and heard what sounded like someone walking down the corridor and the sound of something heavy being dragged on the floor. They immediately ran out into the hallway to investigate, but no one was there. In fact, they were the only people visiting Fort Mifflin that early on in the day.

We were told by Wayne, our trusty guide at Fort Mifflin, that women with blonde hair have felt very uneasy and have had the sensation of their hair being pulled in this particular casement. There were even times, when blondes have come out screaming. We have a few blondes in the group, but no one reported any feelings that their hair was pulled, just a general feeling of malaise and uneasiness.

Our investigation moves on to the Commanding Officer's Quarters. As we open a door to a back room, we are all overwhelmed by the smell of pipe tobacco. We conducted our investigation and got some interesting EMF readings ranging from around 4 to 5, that seemed to move around.

While wandering around outside in the evening the air seems thick and, "Ewww bugs!" I said. Mosquitoes are a bit rampant in the warm summer air. I jumped as a bat flew overhead and it scared the crap out of us. Sure I've been known to shriek and even cry about bats, just ask my mother….My mind rushes and I flail my flashlight around. "C'mon ghosties, come out come out where ever you are…," I whisper quietly.

There have been reports that the specters of soldiers have been seen on the fields, but I don't see any… "All I want is a darn picture of one of these dudes," I say softly to the wind, and one of my teammates giggles. As we traverse quietly, and I continue to snap photos, my camera battery goes dead. Fortunately, I have extra batteries, so I quickly put them in, and they go dead, too. "Hmmmm, okay…," I say quietly.

Quite often, as a spirit is about to manifest, it will draw upon an energy source, and since all my batteries have mysteriously been drained, I am feverishly looking for the ghostly source. Others' batteries are going dead too. It has been a long night, but we have replenished our cameras with new batteries just recently. Because each one of us has opened new packs of batteries and have thrown them in quickly, I keep looking to make sure I put the batteries in correctly. Sure enough I have.

We have conducted some EVP work and have been logging our findings with other equipment, such as our EMF detectors and our digital compass, which tells us time and temperature. We fervently attempt more photos amongst gasps of swears and sighs because our equipment does not seem to be working properly, due to our new batteries mysteriously draining. We are close to the end of our investigation, and we hear the final call on our walkie talkie, its time to head back to base.

Some of our teammates have done investigations here on their own, as well as this one. Two of our members report that as they were holding a vigil in casemate five that they heard the sound of something being dragged down the hallway. However, when they proceeded to peek into the hallway, no one was there…they were alone, supposedly…

Lots Goin' On!

Fort Mifflin is home to several apparitions—two of which include a faceless soldier and Elizabeth Pratt. Elizabeth Pratt is the otherwise known "screaming woman." Apparently police have actually been called out to the grounds of Fort Mifflin because someone has heard a woman screaming. When the police arrive, there is no woman to be found.

There are also reports of a little girl, an old lamplighter, and a blacksmith.

In November of 2006, founder of United States Ghosts Chasers and prior Director of Operations and Photo/Video Analyst for the Maryland Paranormal Investigator, Robbin Van Pelt was invited by The Chester County Paranormal Research Society to attend an investigation at this historical location. An ghost expert in research and electronics, Robbin remembers:

It was hard for me to find my way there in the dark; it is somewhat hidden along side the Philadelphia airport. My first impression of the Fort was very interesting—I was expecting a large location similar to that of Fort McHenry in Baltimore, but what I saw before me actually was, for me, diminutive in stature. I was standing in the parking lot and the only thing I could see was a tall wall with a gated entrance.

Our night began by walking through an underpass; something like a small tunnel. As we emerged on the other side, it was like stepping back in time—a land before my time that is. You could feel a change in the air, an essence from the past. The night was very cold and crisp, a night for gloves, hats, and scarves.

I was coming into this investigation cold. This is a term paranormal investigators use to describe a lack of knowledge of a location or event, when we know nothing about where we are or what has happened there. I prefer to go in this way so I have no bias or prejudgments of a place to influence my experiences.

Mark and Katharine Sarro, the founders of CCPRS, were running the investigation this night. They started us out by dividing us into teams of about five or so—I think we had less than twenty people altogether for the night. We split into teams and went our separate ways.

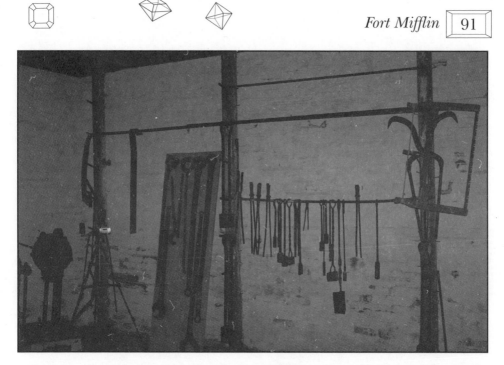

Interior of the blacksmith's shop in Fort Mifflin. *Photo by Katharine Sarro*

My team's first investigation location was Casement #5. The casements were bombproof shelters that were used as prison cells during the war. It was dark as we ventured through the tunnels; you could hear the echo of sounds as we walked. These are things investigators make note of for future reference when going through the evidence at a later time. As we sat in the casement, you could faintly hear the planes and boats going by—another note you would take down for later.

We sat in the dark and turned our audio recorders on to begin an EVP (Electronic Voice Phenomena) session. As we asked our questions, we kept watch on our EMF (Electromagnetic Field) meters and temperature readings. Part way into the EVP session, we kept hearing a light banging sound. I left my seat and walked to the entrance of the casement following the sound. Each time I got close to the sound, it would stop. I walked all the way outside, to the front of the building, to make sure no one else was around to cause the noise. With that a wind came blowing by and I heard the noise again. It was the flagpole. The metal piece on the string was blowing against the metal pole causing it to echo through the tunnels.

After that was solved, we began to hear someone walking in front of the casement and then the steps just ending. Again, I got up to investigate. This time I could not find the cause. I stood at the doorway and heard the footsteps walk towards me and just vanish in front of me—with no one there. We also started smelling cigar smoke for which we found no explanation.

I walked from the casement with the group heading towards the powder magazines. As we were walking past the bathrooms and nearing the gated entrance area, I was hit in the face and chest with a huge blast of hot air. It was like someone had turned on a large heater and aimed it right at me. I have experienced cold spots in haunted locations before, but not a hot spot such as this. I had a person on each side of me and neither Carol nor Ruth felt the hot air. As we started walking again, I kept feeling like something was touching my face and head—like when you walk into a cobweb; again no one else felt this.

We proceeded to the powder magazine area and tried to do some EVP testing. As we were asking questions of the spirits, Carol's watch reset itself to military time and the compasses we were using started to spin; they could not find north. The EMF meters also started to pickup readings. With that, I checked my Natural TriField Meter. It was also picking up a reading. But…just as quick as the readings appeared, they also vanished.

Our next location for investigating was the Officers' Quarters. We began our EVP session. As we listened carefully, we started to hear female voices with our own ears. I assumed it was the another group—they were supposed to be at the far end of the fort, not near us. I walked down from the second floor and went outside to look around. I checked around the building and I even went back to the powder magazine to see if someone had strayed from the other group. I found no one.

I returned to the upstairs floor of the quarters and resumed the EVP session. As we started, we could hear the women speaking again. This time we radioed down to Mark and verified where everyone else was. No one was around us. We couldn't explain it.

Our night at Fort Mifflin ended. I was intrigued and confused by the night. I am a skeptic at heart, and I like being able to find where the sounds come from and be able to explain what has happened. I couldn't that night.

I think Fort Mifflin has a lot activity yet to be explored and investigated.

So what were the strange sensations felt by this seasoned investigator? What caused the steps and voices and movement of air? Surely something was there…. somewhere…sometime…

Sit outside at Fort Mifflin to enjoy the sights— and maybe a few ghosts will be meandering about as well!
Photo by Katharine Sarro

A creepy Fort Mifflin. *Digitized image courtesy of Robbin Van Pelt*

One of the CCPRS investigators, Dinah, says,

Though nothing personally happened to me to indicate that a ghost was tagging along as we moved around the fort the night I attended an investigation, the whole time I felt the tingle of being watched from the darkness. At one point, against group policy, I wandered outside the investigation base—alone—to see if I could identify the feelings of…discomfort…in the air. There was something that was there, but not. Cold, yet warm on the summer breeze. Though alone, I was not alone. Fort Mifflin, in its ghostly elegance, is a force in itself to be reckoned with. But never alone.

If I were to suggest a place for you to begin your quest of *Philadelphia Haunts*…it just might be here…

Chapter Six
Anonymous Spooky Stories

One Weird Thing After the Next!

There are many ghost stories in the grand town of Philadelphia that span the ages. But *old city* does not necessary translate only to *old ghosts*. There are definitely some contemporary stories to be told. These are just a few.

Story One: Home Sweet Home

When I first moved to Philadelphia, there were some renovations being done in the place where I was living. A guest room was constructed during my stay and I eventually ended up occupying that room for a bit. I would wake up in the morning with a smack on my butt and a whisper, "Its time to get up now; c'mon its time to go riding."

I thought my father was walking in his sleep or being silly, so I jumped up to grab him, but he wasn't there! No one was. I opted not to tell my father right away because I did not want to freak him out.

Then there was the clock. Right outside of the guest room was my Grandfather's clock, which would mysteriously wind all on its own. My father was upset with me because he thought that I was winding it. I told him that I wasn't, and he would shrug his shoulders and mutter a *humph* under his breath.

One day, I was trying to get a nap in before going in for my late shift at work, and the door knob to my room was rattling around. I jumped up and swung open the door to see nothing there, but I was shivering from being freezing cold all of a sudden. This made me think that I was sick, because I couldn't stop shaking, I was so cold. I wasn't sick, though… It was summer, but I had been careful to not get a sunburn, I had no sunburn. I took my temperature and it was totally normal. So I jumped in the shower to warm up. Bundling up, I made some hot tea and went to work.

At work I was fine, no shaking from the cold, it was actually quite hot outside. When I spoke with my father the next morning, he asked about the clock again, and again I told him that I had not touched it. I told him how cold it was. And I said in a silly way, "Please don't wake me up at 5:30 in the morning when you know I get home *sooooooooooo* late, plus my butt hurts from that spank—it's not like I'm four years old."

He looked at me like I was crazy…well; I was a kind of a *Goth* kid, so he did have some reason behind the weird way he looked at me.

My father has this huge red chair that I've always loved to curl up in. I have always felt very comforted in this chair. Sometimes while curling up there, I'd feel a tap on my head, I'd look around thinking my father was being goofy, but he traveled so much, and I would remember that I was all alone, that my father was in Italy.

Once in awhile, I'd feel like someone was tugging on my socks; my feet would be so cold, I'd scrunch them up underneath me. One day my father saw me curled up in the chair and made a silly comment, "You know your

Grandfather loved that chair; are you sure you should have your feet up in it?" I gave him a questioning look and asked him why I shouldn't have my "feet up in it." He just laughed and walked out of the room. Until that day, I had no idea that was my Grandfather's favorite chair.

My Grandmother had an unfortunate battle with Alzheimer's disease. I would care for her as much as I could, and we had in-home help for awhile, but it got to be so much to handle. I started to realize that she was carrying on full conversations with someone that I never saw.

One day, as I stood outside of her room, I heard a man answering back, but they were speaking in Portuguese—a language I know bits and pieces of, mostly swear words, unfortunately! I thought one of our Brazilian friends had come in unannounced and I wanted to say hi. I knocked on the door and I heard my grandmother say in English, "Come on in."

I walked in the room and she was alone. I looked around and thought my friend was going to jump out and scare me, but he was honestly not there. I looked everywhere, under the bed, in the bathroom, the closet, under clothes—you get the picture. My grandmother was giggling and said, "Come, come, my dear girl. You will go with him some day, won't you?"

I paid no mind to it because she said a lot of odd things because of the Alzheimer's disease. Then I got a phone call from one of my friends regarding an unfortunate accident that had happened to a guy I had met a few weeks prior. He was Brazilian, spoke Portuguese, and I was so upset to find out that he had been killed in a car accident. I was used to soothing my Grandmother and taking care of her. I went to her to see if she needed anything. I noticed a chill around her and she was shivering. I tucked her in to bed. She tapped my hands and said, "Dear, dear girl go with him."

I thought she had brushed my hair back but, it came from behind me, so I turned to look. I saw nothing, but felt chilled; I was all goosepimply. I turned back to her and felt a tug on my left hand. She said the same thing again. I thought I was losing my mind.

I left the room to sink into a big comfy chair and cry. Through my tears, I kept hearing water running. I checked on my Grandmother and she was fast asleep. I went in the kitchen and the water was running; I turned it off. I still heard water running; it was running in the bathroom sink. I turned that off. The TV turned itself on and started flipping through channels without me doing a thing. I thought something was on top of the remote. I looked at the TV and the remote was on top of it. It stopped on a program about the paranormal and the supernatural. I sat there amazed, excited, and curious about what had just happened.

We had an old typewriter that hadn't been used since the forties that sat out decoratively. Every once in awhile, I'd wake up and hear clicking. I would walk into the living room and that typewriter would be clicking. I thought a key was stuck. I thought, "Oh God, here we go with *The Shining*…or something weird!" My boyfriend at the time heard the clicking one night, walked into the living room and started laughing nervously. He came back into the bedroom and asked, "Where is your grandmother?" I told him that she had passed away recently. He looked at me and said, "Then who is the woman in the living room?"

I was hanging out with my boyfriend when, all of a sudden, we both saw this immense shadow looming over us. I thought, *maybe it's a spider.* I got up and stood on the chairs to look and saw no spiders and no cobwebs. But then it was suddenly freezing. The water turned on by itself in the kitchen. I went into the kitchen and turned it off. Unexpectedly, the glass water container fell to the floor and smashed; water and glass was all over the place.

We cleaned up the mess, turned off the TV, and my boyfriend began writing down ancient prayers in a language I was not familiar with. He prayed. I prayed my own prayers. It was as if this shadow was crawling all over the ceiling. It got so cold we could see our breath and kept saying prayers.

My boyfriend, who had dabbled in the arts of the occult, had made a witches bottle, and he buried it somewhere outside. Once he came back inside we looked up at the night sky. It was so beautiful, so many stars were out, and then we saw an odd looking star that was flashing in thousands of different colors. I thought it was a plane at first, but it wasn't moving at all. We both shivered; we were shaking with cold; it seemed the colors changed in the star as we shook, and could see our breath again. It was not cold. I had turned off the air-conditioning earlier. It was summertime…

Story Two: Locust Street

I was walking home with a good friend when we locked eyes with a distraught man. He was soaking wet and had red splattered on his clothes—it looked

like blood. I was concerned that he was injured, so my friend and I began to talk to him. As we were walking along with this poor drenched soul, he told us that he had just jumped off a bridge in an attempt to kill himself. He then explained that he had just found his son in bed with his girlfriend and was so furious that he killed them both and then tried to kill himself by jumping off the bridge.

My friend and I looked at each other quizzically, *How does a man jump off that bridge and survive?* We got to the corner of 4th and South Street. I remember physically holding his arm and then giving him a hug. While I was doing this, I heard a group of girls crossing 4th Street saying, "Now, just what are *these* freaks doing?" "There's no one there..." "What the...that's right hug the air....ya freak!"

Since Cyrus, our new friend, said that he felt "kinda better," he said he was going to head home, and maybe stop off at his favorite bar. As my friend and I watched him walk down 4th Street, we looked at each other and shook our heads in disbelief. I have since married that friend of mine and he and I still talk about Cyrus. Was that the last hug that he ever received?

Story Three: The Roses

An anonymous source told me an interesting Philadelphia story:

Her grandmother was ill and she and her family had gone to church to pray for her often. One of the many prayers was a prayer to Padre Pio. Her Grandmother began to get better and was able to move around easier, however, due to old age, she had simply passed away in her sleep. She remembers seeing her with her rosary beads hanging from the mantle of her bed.

A few days after the funeral, she and her family were cleaning and putting things away that belonged to her Grandmother. She took the rosary beads from the mantle and noticed a beautiful smell of roses, but there were no roses around.

She thoughtfully prayed for her Grandmother and cried because she missed her so much. As she looked over in the corner of the room, she noticed the curtains billowing, but they had closed all the windows earlier so bugs wouldn't get in. As she walked over to the curtain, she felt a cold chill pass right through her, and again she smelled the roses. When something glittered on the floor, she bent down to take a look. It was her Grandmother's necklace with her cross. She picked it up and started crying again because she said the "feelings were incredibly overwhelming." Deciding to place the rosary beads back on the mantle, she put the necklace in a small box to keep it safe. This, after all, was what the spirit wanted her to do…

Story Four: The Monk

Another story involving a prayer to Padre Pio, only this anonymous source had a different encounter…

Unfortunately, she had been diagnosed with a cancerous cyst on her cervix and was terrified. She had gone to a family dinner where her husband's grandmother said a prayer to Padre Pio in her honor. That night when she got home, she kept smelling roses, but that was just the beginning of her provocative tale.

She began noticing chills late at night and could not fall asleep at all. Just as she thought she had fallen asleep, she smelled the roses again and looked up to see a man clothed in a long brown robe walking across the room. He stopped near her side of the bed; he had a rosary in one hand and a crucifix in the other. He bent over her and she said he whispered, "It's not your time yet."

She then confided in me something incredibly sad; she said that she had attempted to take her own life several times throughout her life because of horrible times of depression caused by some terrible traumas too personal and terrifying to mention here. She went on to tell me, "The weird thing is, he said to me: Not even *you* can change your destiny by ending your life by your own hand, my dear; happiness will be yours, trust in it and believe in it." Interestingly, when she went back to the doctor for a follow-up visit, the cyst and the cancerous cells had miraculously disappeared.

Story Six: The Prayer

The power of prayer has been shown to help uplift and help people in their time of need and even cause a few miracles to happen. A young woman told me that a friend of hers had heard about a sick young lady and she had decided to say a little prayer for her as she was driving by her house one day. The strange thing is, the sick young woman got better and went to the house of the woman who had prayed for her while driving by. She knocked on the door, and as the door opened, she said, "Thank you so much for praying for me; I saw your prayer."

The woman who answered the door looked at this young lady quizzically and soon realized this was the sick young lady she had heard about. They had never actually met before; she'd felt compassion without knowing her. This was the first they had ever met, and now they are close friends.

Chapter Seven
South Philly

South Philly Steaks

One of my most favorite things about Philly? Cheese steaks! On the corner of 9th and Passyunk are two amazing places, Geno's and Pat's Steaks. It just so happens that a gentleman that some refer to as "the coolest guy," like "the Fonze" was nicknamed "Steaks" because he lived overlooking both Pat's and Geno's. Apparently, he had a thing for racing his 57 Chevy, and he would diligently wash and wax it every Friday and then race on Delaware Avenue on Friday night.

Fortunately *Steaks* won his last race, but most *unfortunately* lost his life when his brakes failed—as he ran into a tractor trailer. Once in awhile, one can catch a glimpse of *Steaks* wearing his black leather jacket, with his hair in that cool 60s pompadour style, standing on the corner looking at Pat's and Geno's.

Saint Maria Goretti High School

At the Saint Maria Goretti High School, students and teachers report the feeling of cold hands upon them, a ghost is seen roaming through the halls, and even a statue seems to cry at least once a year!

Stories from the Streets...and Behind the Scenes

Why Can't You See Me?

A young anonymous woman confided her creepy story to me:

One day, I was walking to the grocery store in South Philly and I saw this young lady looking very upset. She was standing on the opposite side of the street outside a door and screaming, "Why can't you see me? C'mon, let me in!" No one came to the door to let her in, so I assumed no one was home. I kept walking, thinking nothing of it. The next thing I knew she was on my side of the street and walking towards me. Her eyes were so sad and she looked so confused. I turned around to try and console her and she was gone.

The weird thing is, when I got to the store, I thought I saw her with a cart, so I walked over to her, only to find an empty cart and no one around. I thought maybe she ran down one of the aisles to get something and left her cart, I waited for a little bit, but she never reappeared. The cart sat there for a long time, empty…"

Ghostly Rentals

When one of my friends suggested that I move in with him at his house in South Philadelphia, I was excited—but also very nervous. He had had a hard time with his prior roommates. My friend told me that when he first moved in, he had only stayed in the house for days, when visiting friends came to find that he had changed drastically. A normally vivacious young man had become a shut in.

In fact, the night before I moved in, he was all alone in the house, and he had some really bizarre experiences. He said that he was continuously woken up by the sound of footsteps running up the stairs and then pushing the door into his room; his door was opening and closing all night long. He said that his dog was twitching and whining all night as well, as if something was incessantly bothering her. There were shadows looming and circling all over his room and over his bed.

One of the first nights there, I was sitting with my new roommates watching TV, and we heard clanking coming from the kitchen, yet no one was in the kitchen. Another night while watching TV, we were startled by a resounding loud thump from the basement. I remember being woken up at three in the morning by the sound of a sledge hammer hitting the concrete in our basement. I ran downstairs and was horrified to hear it even louder.

But when I went back upstairs, all of my roommates were asleep. Nervous we had an intruder, I was ready to dial 911. I crept back down the stairs and cracked the basement door open, turned on the light—and no one was there.

Another night, my other roommates heard the same noise. In fact, when we heard it, one of them went downstairs and just sat there listening to the thudding sound. I should mention that our neighbors to the right were tiny little elderly women all hunched over with horrible osteoarthritis, and to the left, an elderly woman with breast cancer and her husband with Parkinson's disease. It was not likely that they were wielding a hammer of any size.

There were nights while I was trying to fall asleep that I would hear people in the hallway. They were mumbling, but their accents sounded like those of gangsters. I thought one of the TVs was on and got up to turn it off. I opened the door and was chilled to see that the televisions were not on.

Our relationship with our landlord left little to be desired. We had some major issues to complain about, like the water from the shower falling through the dining room ceiling, former tenants had punched in walls and torn the door frame. One of my roommates had purposefully taken the day off from work when our landlord was supposed to come, but he never showed up.

Instead, he surprised me by showing up while I was getting ready for work and my other roommates were already *at* work. As I showed him the damages upstairs from the hole in the wall and the torn door frame to the hole in the floor in the bathroom, we heard a crash downstairs. We ran downstairs; the broom, which was near the cellar, was now in the middle of the floor.

Now, he sees the damage in the ceiling in the dining room and shrugs. I show him the basement; the washing machine is old and not working. Just then we hear another crash, it's the broom again, and it's now in the kitchen. Our Landlord leaves abruptly muttering, "Someone's mad at me…."

I have since learned that our landlord had lived there with his partner who passed away from AIDS. Apparently, he did not die in the house, but this was his favorite house. Quite often, I would hear someone running to the bathroom in the middle of the night; I always assumed it was one of my roommates. I learned it was never a *living* roommate…

Attracting Strange Roommates

Talk about problems with roommates…and friends—we had some doozies! Who knew that the energy around us and in the house could attract such people or turn those once nice into something far more negative? I now see that it's all hooked together. One roommate was one of our best friends; he had moved in with his partner. Once they moved in, they started having problems, and we found out that one was cheating on the other. Their fights were horrible. Since living together, we have lost touch and are no longer friends.

Another roommate was an older gentleman who I found fondling my underclothes and made incredibly rude and disgusting comments. He was a smoker and would light his cigarette using the stove. He left the stove on and the house was full of gas when I got home from work one day. I opened all the windows and rescued our pets. Needless to say, he was not invited back to stay.

Another roommate was an unfortunate con-artist who caused a lot of problems with our family and our friends.

My husband and I argued a lot before we got married. In fact, the night before we were to hop on a plane to our eloping destination, there was a knock on the door at three in the morning that we opted to ignore! (More ghosts?)

When I found myself out of a job and at home much more, with no roommates, I got the full onslaught of the house. This is when I began to understand. I would see a tiny figure of a woman in a long white veil coming down the stairs. The cat would sit and stare at the stairs. I'd see the cat playing all by herself, pawing at the air and rolling on her back to expose her cute pink belly. Was this apparition the negative influence? I don't know.

Things became a bit disconcerting when I kept hearing growling. I'd search out all the cats and the dog, and none of them were making the noise. I used to blame them for being stinky because I smelled this horrible smell of sulfur—it was just disgusting.

One day, while home and waiting for the phone to ring from all of my numerous job applications, I was watching *The Amityville Horror* on TV. It got me thinking about all the weird things in our house. Not that it was anything like the movie, but I started to wonder about things a bit more. I decided to contact a paranormal group and ask some questions.

Instead, they asked *me* a lot of questions and put me in contact with a demonologist—not quite what I expected. I thought maybe they would come and set up equipment and either prove or disprove what was happening. They said that they did not want to cause any further disturbance in the home that I was living in. My best line of defense was to be strong in my faith. In fact, I was told by the demonologist that Mr. Lutz, who had lived in the house in Amityville, turned to religion after his experience and it was hoped that I would do the same. My faith, at the time, was wavering, and I was incredibly insecure.

I was told to keep a log of events in the house, everything from cold spots, to chills, and seeing any of the apparitions—every minute detail I was told to record. So I did just that, and that's when I saw patterns that became incredibly interesting, and frightening. I had been doing research on the paranormal and different types of hauntings.

Along with my paranormal research, I was searching for religion. I was brought up without a strict religious connection, so I felt like I needed something; I just did not know what. When I had to go into the hospital a few years prior for a series of tests, I had bought a book on Buddhism to read while I was there. Now I was searching all over for this book. Strangely, I ended up stubbing my toe on it because it had fallen off of the bookshelf—I considered this the wake up call that I needed.

I turned to Buddhism and began lighting incense and reciting mantras. Though I was nervous at first, the more I did this, the more different the house felt. My husband remarked that the house felt "lighter" somehow.

I did more digging, looking into my own family history, because I had remembered a chant that my Grandmother had taught me when I was four years old. I looked it up and found that it was an ancient chant translated from Gaelic. Unfortunately, my grandmother passed away when I was about five years old, so I couldn't exactly ask her about these things happening to me.

I used the chant that she had taught me all those years ago, though, and I still use it! As you can imagine, due to my family history, I have inherited a propensity for the paranormal. There has even been another family member who was intrigued and fascinated to the point of going to India to study meditation and the paranormal. She wanted to contact a loved one and was absolutely desperate in her attempt. Unfortunately, it may be that it was her desperation that kept her from being able to contact him.

In all the research I have done, I have learned that the sheer anxiety and desperation of wanting to contact a deceased loved one can actually hinder the process of being able to contact the "other side." The same applied with my desire to contact my Grandmother and one of my very first best friends who had died from leukemia. I have been unable to contact either one of their spirits successfully. At any rate, my situation held me in its grip and I sought help; one psychic told me that both my grandmother and my friend had already been reborn, and that they would find a way back into my life.

The good news was that my research drew me closer to figuring out what was, in fact, happening around me and in our house. My exploration into my family history revealed that my Grandmother had exercised an old Celtic practice, and even more astonishing, it was also revealed that on my maternal Grandfather's side, magick had been used. This gave me a double whammy, so to speak.

I panicked a bit because even I had dabbled in this arcane art, and I wondered if what was happening was some sort of repercussion. I have been informed that, due to my own history, it was possible that discarnate energies would surface because of this old religious practice of magic.

The intriguing thing is this: Now that we live in a different home—away from our Philadelphia home— and the same things are happening in this home. The bathroom has a leak through the dining room ceiling to the dining room floor. There has even been the smell of sulfur, which I really wish I could blame on my stinky husband or the cats or the dog. No growling, but I constantly have the feeling that I am being watched. Where we live now, there is constant construction around us, and we live in a very historical area. Do negative energies follow families or people?

We had conducted some paranormal investigations within our current house to decipher the goings on. Our discussions with John Zaffis (demonologist) have been intriguing, and he has suggested that we discontinue our investigations in this new house just outside the Philly area. There is an interesting phenomenon classified as discarnate energies and demons. Unbeknownst to me for awhile, now I know they do exist. It is a level of paranormal activity which is intriguing, however, quite frightening at the same time.

I have been informed by my trusty sources that I need to let go of my fear, because it is that very fear that allows the energy to grow. These discarnate energies feed off of fear, negativity, and insecurity in one's faith. That is why the demonologist who I had been first put into contact with asked me about my faith. I admitted to him that I was confused. I was reading passages from the Bible at that time. In essence what I was doing was declaring war with whatever energy was manifesting or had already manifested in the house.

As I researched Buddhism, I found that there were specific demons, specific Tibetan mantras, and rites that someone like me should not practice. I panicked at first because I did not know who on earth to contact to help us, but I found that, as my own personal beliefs began to settle into Buddhism, the negativity in the house began to dissipate. I had begun meditating, using a personal mantra given to me long ago, and I began using incense.

When I was young, I spoke with a very distinguished man who spoke to me about Buddhism. This is why I

have always been incredibly fascinated by the Buddhist religion. As the house cleared of its negativity, my husband noticed a radical difference. Not only did the house "feel different," but our lives had begun to take a turn for the better. I actually got a job, and my work was being praised and respected—I was simply astonished.

Chapter Eight
Odd and the Bizarre Facts
about Philadelphia

Bram Stoker

Throughout the late 1800s, Bram Stoker traveled through the United States on tour with the Lyceum Theatre. In fact, Bram Stoker wrote a page of notes on his famous *Dracula* on Bellvue-Stratford Hotel stationary. The Rosenbach Museum has contained a collection of notes which he comprised regarding the novel. A majority of this famous work was actually researched and worked on while he was in Center City Philadelphia. The *Dracole Waida*, a pamphlet which Bram Stoker used as a source of information, also remains in the Rosenbach Museum.

For more information, contact, Rosenbach Museum and Library, 2008-2010 Delancey Place, Philadelphia, Pennsylvania 19103; telephone 215-732-1600; web site www.rosenbach.org.

The Mutter Museum

The Mutter Museum is, without a doubt, one of the oddest museums one will ever step into. The museum displays a variety of medical oddities including bizarre things in jars, organs which are diseased, and deformed bones. There is a tumor that was removed from President Grover Cleveland's jaw, and even the thorax from Lincoln's assassin, John Wilkes Booth! Although there are accounts of seeing the ghost of the "Soap Lady" at Eastern State Penitentiary, her real body is easily visible here at the Mutter Museum.

For more information, contact the College if Philadelphia Mutter Museum at 19 South 22nd Street, Philadelphia, Pennsylvania 19103-3097; telephone 215-563-3737; web site http://www.collphyphil.org/mutter.

The Philadelphia Experiment

There is the speculation that an alleged Navy experiment was conducted in Philadelphia that rocked the nation. The Philadelphia Experiment (otherwise known as Project Rainbow) was performed on October 28, 1943. It supposedly consisted of making the USS *Eldridge* dematerialize and become invisible, and teleporting from Philadelphia to Norfolk, Virginia, and back. Apparently, the side effects caused the sailors not only to become invisible, but unfortunately, they are said to have gone crazy as well. The Navy allegedly quit using this technology based on Einstein's unified field theory.

The Cave of Kelpius

A German immigrant named Johannes Kelp became known to his followers as Kelpius the Mystic. The cave is where Kelpius spent his days meditating alone, and still stands in the Wissahickon. His followers comprised a brotherhood of men who called themselves by a few names, one of which was the "Woman of

Wilderness," which was named after a character in the Bible's *Book of Revelation*. These mystics stayed in the wilderness and totally avoided the city. Their practices included meditation, magic, medicine, music, astrology, numerology, and alchemy. The mystics watched for signs of the "impending Rapture." The cave can be found near Hermit Lane. There have been claims that six men wearing brown hooded robes are seen walking through the woods near Forbidden Drive.

The Curious Case of Katie King

The spiritualist movement began in the Nineteenth Century after the twins Margaret and Kate Fox told anyone and everyone that they could communicate with the dead. In July of 1874, at the Holmes' residence, several had gathered to participate in the summoning of a spirit from a "cabinet." This "cabinet" was a piece of equipment used by spiritualists during a séance. After a session of chanting, the guests were shocked to see a beautiful young lady mysteriously appear to be stepping out of the cabinet. This young lady is known as Katie King. She seemed to have appeared out of thin air…had she, or hadn't she?

A respected German Scientist was involved in another session where Katie King had made an appearance. He deduced that the young lady in question was, in fact, a fraud involved in a money-making scheme, and was able to back it up. Apparently, Katie was not her real name, but rather Annie Morgan—and not a ghost at all.

The Curse of William Penn

It was assumed that the statue of William Penn on top of City Hall would stay the highest point in Philadelphia based on the "gentlemen's agreement."

In 1974 and 1975, The Flyers were reigning champions, The Phillies scored a big win in 1980, and, in 1983, The Sixers won the NBA title.

Unfortunately, everything changed in 1984 when Liberty One was built 450 feet higher than Mr. Penn, and then Liberty Two soon followed. Apparently angered, William Penn placed a curse on the city that the sports teams would fail consistently.

Philly sports fans beware…Respect for Mr. William Penn may be the key to our sports teams' success or failure. I wouldn't suggest demolishing Liberty One or Two, just don't dress William up in Eagles Garb! This humble Quaker has not taken too kindly to colorful sportswear in the past!

Chapter Nine
Haunted Cemeteries and Mansions

Palmer Cemetery

Palmer Cemetery, located on Palmer and Belgrade Streets in Philadelphia, is the home of some odd apparitions including that of someone tall holding a baby staring out of the fence, shadows running and milling around, and even that of a young teenage boy hanging from a tree. There are reports that when visiting their departed loved ones, people have had the sensation of being watched. In fact, after having left flowers at the graves, those flowers mysteriously vanish, when mourners have turned their backs for a moment.

Leverington Cemetery

Located at Ridge and Lyceum, Leverington Cemetery has been home to apparitions on a frequent basis. In this Forest Hills cemetery, a ghost of a man dressed in a tuxedo is seen wandering the grounds. Could he be in search of his lovely bride, or merely interested in the exquisite night life of Forest Hills?

An old grave located in the Old Pine Street Presbyterian Church. *Photo by Katharine Sarro*

Mount Moriah Cemetery

This cemetery, located in Southwest Philadelphia along Cobbs Creek, was on March 26, 1855, incorporated in Philadelphia, and sprawled over fifty-four acres of land. The entrance to Mount Moriah Cemetery is ornate and Romanesque, and its brownstone gatehouse is located on Islington Lane, today known as Kingsessing Avenue. There are several accounts of strange ghostly encounters within the gates of Mount Moriah—some chilling to this day.

Chased by a Ghost

Many years ago, the area within the Mount Moriah Cemetery by the great anchor monument served as a teen hangout. This one particular night, several local teens decided to spend the evening there—to let off some steam. One young man, sitting on the edge of the anchor, was staring off down the hill—he saw something. Another asked, "What are you staring at?"

"Look," said the young man. He pointed down the hill to two tall trees situated close together. "Watch there; between the trees. Something just moved behind that one tree."

They all stared. In seconds, they all saw a tall (about seven feet tall!) wispy, cloudy…thing… move from behind one tree and then to the other. They couldn't tell what it was—only that it looked like a tall thin, smoky, ghost-like creature. The boys continued to watch, becoming nervous now.

Seconds passed and the ghost suddenly—as though seeing them clearly now—started to move up the hill towards them.

Now *that* scared them! They scattered, and all jumped into the car. Oddly, though, (and scary) the car would not

A well-attended portion of the Mount Moriah Cemetery. *Photo by Dinah Roseberry*

start—the engine just clicked and sputtered. All the teens were yelling at the driver to get them out of there before the ghost got any closer. They rolled up all the windows as the driver continued to try to start the car—all while the ghost, more quickly now, was moving up the hill.

Finally, the car started and the teens peeled out of there—spinning dust and dirt as they went. Unfortunately, the dirt road they were on wound back around to where the ghostly image had started up the hill near the trees. When it saw them take off, it changed direction and quickened its pace. It was still pursuing them! At the rate it was going and at the rate the car was traveling, the ghost would intercept them before the cutoff that would take them out of the cemetery.

The boys were screaming now. What was it? Why was it following them? And, of course, *faster, faster*!

They *did* beat the ghost out of the cemetery that night—though just barely—and got away, seeing it behind them hovering in the road right after they passed.

The boys had not been back, until now, when one returned to recount his story to me many years later!

A New Cemetery Visit

Three members of the Chester County Paranormal Research Society joined the now older man, who'd seen the willowy ghost many years before. It was a windy fall day, bright sunshine lighting the cemetery and taking away any fears of night terrors that may have lingered from past associations.

The anchor was still there, but the rolling land that looked clearly to the two trees in question all those years ago was now a forest. The area could no longer be seen from the anchor. So the team took off through the white picket teeth

The anchor area of the cemetery—a beginning point for a teen ghost story many years prior—now overlooks a forest-like area. *Photo by Dinah Roseberry*

tombstones and through the cemetery to get a feel of what had once been.

It was a strange place now, with much of the older parts of the cemetery being overgrown and neglected. Though paths were sometimes clear, trails leading to the past were often grown over with brush and wired-wood fingers. Still there was a beckoning that could not be denied. The cemetery seemed to welcome us into its clutches.

On the way around the paths to find the two trees, where the ghost had been seen all those years ago, there were some strange occurrences. The first dealt with a smell—a very strong sulfur-like odor just as we passed the military section near the anchor, but on a side pathway. And a bit further along, a rather disconcerting cat watched our progress

Here are some tombstones within the sprawling cemetery of Mount Moriah which is located in Southwest Philadelphia. *Photo courtesy of Kim Ritchie*

much like a *familiar* from a bygone witch era. It rushed away through the undergrowth as we came closer, but we all shivered when we saw its peering eyes.

Just a cat...

A macabre scene, complete with cat on a tombstone! *Photo by Dinah Roseberry*

As two investigators moved towards the mysterious "tree area," they stopped suddenly because they could hear voices on the wind and footsteps behind them—rather in between the wind gusts. No one else was around. And they both jumped as a very loud bang reverberated through the area, but the two others on the team, very close by, heard nothing.

Said one investigator, "You know, for a windy day, I was having a lot of audio experiences...I knew it wasn't the wind, though my first thought that it was almost as if the wind might have been 'carrying' the sounds...or simply, amplifying them...There was more than one occasion, I thought I heard multiple voices, but only picked that up one time on my EVPs." Still, it told us that something was afoot.

One of the sensitives of the team finally came upon the trees and felt a malice that was eerie coming from the area. He felt

An overgrown tombstone, still beckons visitors from its hiding place. *Photo by Dinah Roseberry*

Tombstones nearly reclaimed by the landscape. A strange light appeared at the bottom left of the photo showing red and orange in the color version. *Photo by Kim Ritchie*

It was here where one of our team felt incredible discomfort. This area is in direct line, and close by to, the two trees where a ghostly figure was seen many years ago. *Photo by Dinah Roseberry*

An anomalous light of a rainbow appears in the middle of the sky above Mount Moriah on a beautiful sunny day when absolutely no rain fell!
Photo by Kim Richie

that whatever had been there all those years ago, was still in the same place—and had the same issues. There were plans made to return with full equipment to see exactly what was haunting the area. But for now, we left the area to the brush.

And finally, overhead, though there was no rain or moisture on this bright sunshiny day, a perfect rainbow could be seen, it's colors, according to another researcher, in the wrong order. An odd occurrence.

Saint Peter's Church Cemetery

Located on 4th and Pine Street, this cemetery has a few ghosts lurking around the grounds. There are reports of a carriage, Native American Chiefs, and even a Colonial-era

A spooky path at Mount Moriah. *Photo by Katharine Sarro*

Another eerie area at Mount Moriah. *Photo by Katharine Sarro*

gentleman walking through the moonlit graveyard. No one ever walks here alone!

Christ Church Burial Ground

This cemetery dates back to 1719, and is the final resting place of several signers of the Declaration of Independence, and even Benjamin Franklin and his family. It is said that if a coin is thrown on Franklin's grave, it will bring good luck. Benjamin Franklin is said to be seen wandering at dusk through the city streets and can even be spotted lurking around Christ Church near his grave.

His statue, which is actually in front of The American Philosophical Society, is rumored to come to life and dance through the streets of Philadelphia. In 1884, a cleaning woman at the Philosophical Society described being nearly knocked over by Benjamin Franklin...yet how is that possible, if the late Benjamin Franklin lies in his grave at Christ Church Burial Ground?

Philadelphia was plagued with the Yellow Fever in 1793, and it is also rumored that those struck dead by the disease, still lurk amongst the graves in the Burial Ground of Christ Church.

(Note: Please be respectful of these mansion properties as there are privately owned or posted.)

Baleroy Mansion

Baleroy is the home of a few ghosts, which include Thomas Jefferson who likes to appear in the dining room, a kindly Monk who roams in the bedrooms, and an old woman who enjoys swatting at visitors with her cane. And we mustn't forget "Amelia" who is extremely possessive of an old chair, that is reportedly cursed—those who sit in the chair, die soon afterwards.

Even ectoplasm has been reported to ooze from the doorframes of Baleroy.

Loudon Mansion

Loudon Mansion was built over the graves of Revolutionary War Soldiers, and numerous apparitions have been reported. A ghost of a young boy who has been named "Willie" has been seen and it is said that it is he who moves objects and enjoys rearranging books in the library. A lovely young woman has been seen on the front porch and meandering around inside of the house. Photos taken of the Loudon mansion often contain orbs and tall columns of white lights.

Bolton Mansion

The Bolton Mansion allegedly houses the ghosts of a little girl and a woman who appears to be searching for something or someone.

Fonthill Mansion

Fonthill Mansion, located in Fairmount Park, was the home of the Revolutionary War Hero Thomas Mifflin, and his wife. Quite tragically, Mifflin's wife battled with her sanity, went mad, and eventually died in the mansion. There are numerous reports of seeing lights go on in the mansion when no one is there and of a woman walking the halls and surrounding roads of Fonthill.

Lemon Hill Mansion

Lemon Hill, also located in Fairmount Park, was built by Henry Pratt in 1799. Robert Morris, one of the signers of the Declaration of Independence, owned the land. He had greenhouses installed and grew lemons. The lemon trees and greenhouses are long gone; in fact, it's been centuries since they've been there, yet still the scent of lemons will waft through the air, and one can see apparitions and shadows darting about.

Mount Moriah mauselum—creepy. *Photo by Katharine Sarro*

At one entrance to Mount Moriah Cemetery, this area has been known for interesting orbs appearing in photos. On this day, all was quiet. *Photo by Dinah Roseberry*

Appendix One
Paranormal Phenomenon:
Staying Centered and Grounded

The law of attraction also applies to an interest in the paranormal! As one may receive attention from angels and spirit guides in their spiritual journey, other discarnate energies may become attracted as well. Therefore, it becomes imperative to take care and make sure that one protects themselves.

Easy Steps

There are easy steps that will assist you as you center and ground yourself. For example:

- eating properly,
- exercising,
- positive attitudes,
- being outside in nature and taking a walk by a clean river, lake, or the sea, just being in the sun, and even walking near trees all fill us with a sense of well being.

Grounding exercises such as:

- Visualization—visualize that roots have grown from the soles of your feet deep into the earth, or that a large bubble surrounds you like a strong membrane, or even visualizing shields around you can be incredibly grounding and protective.
- Carrying the gemstones hematite, black obsidian, and smoky quartz can help one to feel grounded.
- Even essential oils and incense such as Frankincense, Eucalyptus, and even Juniper can assist in the grounding process.
- Wearing symbols of protection as jewelry can also assist in helping one to feel protected by their faith, a cross, the Star of David, an Ankh, or a pentacle all work well. If you can't afford a piece of jewelry, a representation on a piece of paper also works just as well.

Cleansing exercises include: While showering, imagine that the water is cleansing you of all negativity and all the negativity is flowing down the drain. Additionally, salt is one of the oldest methods of cleansing and works beautifully in a bath.

Symptoms of Negativity

Symptoms that one has been affected by negative energies are:

- Feeling down or angry with no real cause, especially if it is out of one's character,
- Feeling really drained or exhausted for no reason at all,
- Having odd thoughts that are totally out of character, or
- Having feelings of being out of control, and
- Even nightmares.

If there is a suspicion that negative energies have made an imprint, please don't allow fear to take over. Fear will only allow the energies to multiply. Use some of the methods suggested and contact an experienced healer to assist you.

One of my favorite necklaces is obsidian which I use for protection and to block negativity. *Photo by Katharine Sarro*

It is necessary to protect ones self when doing paranormal investigations. We all use different methods of protection. The different methods used can be a combination of prayer, talismans—such as a cross or an ankh or udjat—or even using aromatherapy or gemstones to keep one grounded and centered. Some of our members, including myself, use gemstones and oils to aid in our protection. I like to use obsidian, hematite, rose quartz, citrine, and carnelian. Carnelian is linked with courage, and staying focused in the present moment. Citrine is a protection stone that encourages strength and confidence, and is even said to promote creativity and prosperity. There are many gemstones with intriguing and fascinating properties. I have included a brief list of some interesting facts and properties of gemstones and oils that are often used to promote protection, grounding, centering, and general well being. You may want to enhance your own protection and well-being by using some of the following. These stones and oils can often be purchased in local mind, body, spirit shops, new age retailers, or internet sites dealing with internal—and external!—spirit.

AGATE

A stone of good fortune, health and long life. Said to attract the love of others, increase courage, intelligence, strength and modesty and to benefit the heart. Protection from bad dreams, stress, and energy drains. The blue lace variety is used for its calming effect. Color: Comes in many colors and usually has a banded or striped appearance.

ALEXANDRITE

Alexandrite is known as the "stone of good omen." Alexandrite is used to bring inner peace and magnanimity of heart and to benefit head, spine, neck, eyes, and memory. For healing purposes, it works best on the crown, brow, and solar plexus. A change of color happens depending on the light.

AMAZONITE

For soothing the nervous system, strengthening the meridians, and improving thinking abilities. Healing properties, soothing, works on the throat chakra and instills confidence. Amazonite is known as the stone of "hope" because it helps to instill hope.

AMBER

Technically is not a gemstone, but is the fossilized sap from prehistoric trees. It absorbs negativity so, therefore, needs to be cleansed often. Early physicians prescribed amber for headaches, heart problems, arthritis, and a variety of other ailments. In ancient times, amber was carried by travelers for protection. To early Christians, amber signified the presence of the Lord. In the Far East, amber is the symbol of courage; Asian cultures regard amber as the "soul of the tiger;" Egyptians placed a piece of amber in the casket of a loved one to ensure the body would forever remain whole. Often used as a talisman for courage and self confidence. It calms the nerves, gives confidence, regains memory loss, thyroid, inner ear, and neuro-tissue strengthener, and activates altruistic nature and realization of the spiritual intellect. Amber brings a care free, sunny disposition, promotes good luck and success, assists in dissolving oppositions, helps with stomach, spleen, and kidney ailments, reduces joint problems, and has even been used to alleviate teething pain in babies. Amber imparts sympathy and understanding, healing and attracting. Used for making and breaking spells, for calming and healing, uplifting, and absorbing negative energies from the body. It is said to give children strength if hung around the neck and also to help rheumatism, toothache, headaches, goiter, bleeding, intestine and bladder problems, earache, asthma, bronchitis, throat irritations, and is often carried for luck. Amber is believed also to benefit the performances of actors and actresses, when worn with amethyst.

AMETHYST

For meditation, soothing the mind, and re-balancing the spirit. For protection from negative vibrations, healing and easing pain, purifying blood, and encouraging sleep. It is said to tone down drunkenness. It is traditionally associated with Saint Valentine, a stone of love and friendship and a fortunate gem for lovers and friends. When worn with Carnelian, said to restrain those who are domineering and highly strung.

ALUM

Worn for protection against disease and the *evil eye*.

AQUAMARINE

A stone of joy, hope, love, and spiritual vision. Used for calming the mind, lifting the spirits, and preserving innocence. This is a good stone for seers and mystics and those seeking intelligence and self knowledge. Soothes emotions and nerves, and is healing for eyes, liver, stomach, glands, and swollen feet.

AVENTURINE

Green—healing, blue—uplifting, congestion, circulation.

AZURITE

It is believed to reveal to the owner the purpose of life and open pathways to truth. To aid psychic development and help open the *third eye* center. It encourages sympathy, understanding, and intuition. Azurite is often used in meditation. On the physical level, it is helpful for rebuilding cells, dissolving diseased tissue, and for arthritis, knee problems, and hip pain.

BLACK ONYX

Helps in changing bad habits, and is grounding. It is ideal as a necklace.

BLOODSTONE

(A variety of Jasper). Used for idealism and for strengthening the will to do well. Helps those inclined to extremes, wards off harmful vibrations, calms negative emotions, and encourages a pleasant disposition. Also used to purify blood and detoxify organs (especially liver, kidneys, and spleen) and to help stop bleeding.

BLUE JOHN

Helpful for overworked mediums and other sensitives.

BOWENITE:

(Korean Jade) Helps depression, insomnia, and indigestion. It sharpens spirituality and vision when worn with Chrysoprase. Color: green.

CALCITE

For mental clarity and allaying anxiety, and to aid awareness and intuition. (Many colors.)

CARNELIAN

Is believed to encourage friendship and cheerfulness and to protect from evil, to ground energies, concentration, and strengthen family love. Also used for understanding and vigor, overcoming negativity, bringing wisdom, and combating depression and sluggishness. It is often used for protection from bad vibrations, negativity, and evil, and stabilizes energy within the home. Associated with the Sacral Chakra Helpful for lower spine problems, bleeding, rheumatism, and infertility or impotence, and helps to heal wounds. It strengthens the voice, and is often referred to as "the actor's stone."

CHRYSOCOLLA

For psychic development, meditation, and healing.

CHRYSOLITE
(A kind of topaz.) The stone of astrologers and fortune tellers, believed to attract occult powers, encourage inner vision, tranquility of mind, and ability to see into the future.

CHALCEDONY
For peace, confidence, and cheerfulness, to minimize over sensitivity and protect against the *evil eye*. It is said to help in fever reduction. Color: varies, usually black or green.

CITRINE
Stone of protection which removes and deflects all negativity. Citrine is used for improving confidence and self image, for clarity of thought, cheerfulness, fairness to others and emotional control. It is popularly known as the "success stone" or "merchant's stone" because it assists in promoting prosperity, success, and abundance, and imparting a sense of generosity. It brings about good fortune in unexpected ways. Citrine can clear the air of any negativity. Citrine enhances will power and mental clarity, as well as increasing creativity and promoting honesty. It is also helpful for circulation, toxic conditions, purifying the blood, and for diabetes.

CONAMARA MARBLE
(Celtic green.)Inner peace/freedom from worry.

CRYSTAL
(Quartz) stone of mystics, psychics, and healers. Helps focus, awareness, and meditation, calms mind and eases anxiety and pain. Also helpful for diarrhea, dizziness, kidney problems, spasms, vertigo, hemorrhages. It amplifies the effects of other stones. Has many important uses.

CHRYSOPHRASE
For psychic development, meditation, and healing. A talisman used to bring victory. Aids clear thinking.

CORAL
Believed to protect against witchcraft and the *evil eye* and to draw away melancholia. Also said to dim when the owner is ill, as it absorbs the effects of illness. For anemia, bladder conditions, and joint problems.

DIAMOND
Is used for invoking love and fidelity and bringing courage and longevity. It is also helpful in overcoming enemies, and amplifies the energy of other stones. The diamond is worn on the "heart" finger in marriage to encourage faithfulness and purity of heart—an ancient folk charm that we still use today.

EILAT STONE
(A form of chrysocolla.) A stone highly valued by King Solomon. It is believed to aid intuition, wisdom, and psychic power.

EMERALD
For intelligence, prophecy, business success, emotional stability and understanding. Promotes love and is believed to be a link with divine forces. Used in healing for eye troubles, skin ulcers, insomnia, epilepsy, colds, headaches, asthma, and the pains of childbirth.

FLUORITE
For encouraging positive energies, balancing the energies, opening chakras and strengthening bone tissue.

GARNET
Believed to help in the development of clairvoyance and to help the mind to be pure, hopeful, cheerful, confident, honest, frank, faithful, and sincere. Stimulates the imagination, calms the mind, and helps depression and laziness. Believed also to aid skin problems and strengthen the base of spine. When worn as beads or carried in the pocket, is said to calm over-activity and restlessness, especially in the young. Used as a symbol of remembrance between parting friends. Color: deep claret red.

HELIODORE
For spiritual illumination and for the heart and circulation.

HEMATITE
For courage and endurance, strengthening heart, regulating pulse, and for ulcers, cramps and blood disorders, i.e., anemia, plus inflammation of joints, fatigue, and melancholy (especially during pregnancy). Color: metallic silver gray.

JADE
Believed to be a lucky charm. Used for warding off spirits, safe journeys, wisdom and long life and for slowing down ageing. Brings peace and serenity and is a good for high blood pressure, heart and circulation problems, diabetes and kidney and bladder problems. Color: Green—shades of green vary according to type of jade, (nephrite jade tends to be a mossy olive green).

JASPER
Believed to have magical properties and protect against the *evil eye*, witchcraft, and phantasms. It encourages the person to do good deeds. Also used for improving the sense of smell, calming emotional problems, and guilt feelings, lowering blood pressure and helping kidney, stomach and bladder complaints, biliousness, and epilepsy. Has the power to console. Color: can vary, usually yellow/orange.

JET
General magical and healing properties. To quiet fears, aiding the grieving process (hence its popularity in the mourning jewelry of the Victorian period) and protecting from violence and illness. Used for headaches, toothache, glandular swelling, stomach pains, epilepsy, and hysteria. Jet is considered in to be a powerful magical talisman to ward off negative influences. Color: black.

LAPIS LAZULI:
Said to help in the development of psychic abilities. Aids depression, builds hope and self confidence, and improves health. It is believed to encourage fidelity in love. Helps one to find the inner truth and elevates consciousness. In healing, it is used for heart, spleen, blood and digestive problems, and brain diseases such as epilepsy. An "emotional sanctuary." Color: Deep blue, sometimes with tiny metallic flecks of silica.

MAGNETITE
(Lodestone) for honesty, wisdom, and integrity. It is often used to help postural imbalances of spine and related headaches, rheumatics, neuralgia, liver and eye diseases. Color: gray/black.

MALACHITE
It is often used for raising the spirits, increasing hope, health and happiness, attracting prosperity, and removing blocks to spiritual growth. The copper in malachite is said to help irregular menstruation and this stone is also valued for toothache, asthma, eyesight problems, and rheumatism.

MARBLE
For protection against witchcraft.

MEXICAN ONYX
To aid sleep, and help insomnia.

MOONSTONE
For success, inspiration, and calmness, for reconciling parted lovers, uplifting and balancing emotions, and attracting good things, (believed to ensure a good crop if hung from a fruit tree). It is a good stone for travelers. In India, this was regarded to be a lucky gem if given to a bride by her groom. It is said to be helpful for dropsy and water retention. Peach, for comfort, white for balance and the blue variety is considered best. Color: white, peach/pink, pale blue.

MOSS AGATE
Attunement with nature and growing things.

MOSS OPALITE
Calms temper and nerves, enhances psychic powers, but brings luck only to the pure in heart, as it reflects one's own thoughts back.

MOTHER OF PEARL
For self confidence and attracting friendship. It is also believed to enhance the appearance of the skin.

OPAL
Similar effect to moss opalite. Believed fortunate for Librans, also helpful for lung conditions. Color: varies (multi).

OBSIDIAN:
Can be used for removing blocks to the healing process. Good for divination. Helps to protect the very sensitive against depression, and is the stone for the gentle and soft people of this world. It reveals subconscious, hidden truths, sharpening external and internal vision, helping stomach and improving muscle tone. Color: black or black with white blotches. (Snowflake).

ONYX
Aids thinking, imagination, and decision-making. Also said to promote fidelity and attract fortune. Color: usually green, brown, or black.

PEARL
For endurance and emotional stability and to benefit the lungs. Brings about focus, integrity, purity, faith, spirituality, wisdom, sincerity, fertility, innocence, and charity. Pearls are said to promote endurance and emotional stability and to benefit the lungs. There are some claims that pearls can be used to help tap into one's inner wisdom and even to nurture the growth of love.

PERIDOT
Believed to be favored by the inhabitants of Atlantis. Said to help psychic vision and protect from delusions, to help the timid, balance and uplift the mind, and encourage serenity and trust. Aids muscle function, counteracts some of the effects of alcohol, and is useful for stomach acidity, digestive problems, and calcification. Color: Golden green.

POPPY JASPER
For happiness and encouraging positive energy.

RHODOCROSITE
For integrating physical, emotional, and mental fields, reducing depression and retarding ageing. Inspires forgiveness, and helps owner face reality and new situations.

RHODONITE:
Helps lessen worry, depression irritability, confusion and inconsistency, eases foreboding and disturbing etheric influences. It is ideal for mediums. Helps thyroid function, central nervous system, digestion, and muscles, and when worn on third finger of left hand, is believed to induce compassion and sensitivity to higher values. Color: orange.

ROSE QUARTZ
It is known as the "Love Stone," and is said to bring gentleness, compassion, forgiveness, kindness, and tolerance. This stone is used for enlivening the imagination and calming emotions. Promotes unconditional love, both for ourselves and others, friendship and an appreciation for beauty, hastens recovery, gladdens the heart, and brings inner peace. It heightens self esteem. It is a powerful releaser of unexpressed emotions, and assists in relieving stress and tension. Rose Quartz is believed to ward off harmful vibrations by absorbing them, helpful for aching

bones and bruises and for encouraging recovery from illness. Color: Soft rose pink. It is said that if placed under the pillow, it will draw your dream lover to you; it is also said that it keeps one looking and feeling young.

RUBY
A Buddhist stone, believed to bring intuition and initiative, loyalty and courage, and to protect against loss, unfaithfulness of partner, envy, or nightmares. It forewarns of danger. It is used for pains, spasms, and fevers. Rasputin was said to have used a ruby to heal the Tsar's son who had hemophilia.

RUTILE QUARTZ
Rebalances the different levels of consciousness and also the endocrine glands. It increases tissue regeneration. Good for bronchial sufferers. Used as an aid to mental and psychic activity. Color: clear with gold threads or fibers throughout.

SAPPHIRE
Symbol of truth, associated with saints, yogis, mystics, and healers. Stimulates imagination and brings devotion, faith, and peace, curbs impulsiveness and encourages sympathy. It is also helpful for nervous complaints and asthma. Color: blue.

SMOKEY QUARTZ
Purifies energy centers and has stabilizing effect, especially in material matters where it encourages frugality. Heals and lifts depression and is used to aid psychic ability and meditation. It is said to benefit the abdominal areas, kidneys, pancreas, and sexual organs. Color: transparent Smokey brown.

SODALITE
For courage, endurance, open-mindedness, logic, and rationality, and for bringing light-heartedness, youth, and freshness. It is used to lower blood pressure and fever. This stone is believed to have a healing effect on animals if placed near their domain. Color: Dark blue.

SERPENTINE
To protect from snake bites, also for ulcers, swelling and rheumatism.

SELENITE
For clarifying thoughts and expanding mental powers.

SPINEL
Used to strengthen character, brings idealism and harmony, and decrease stress. Also to promote nerve and muscle function, and aid stomach acidity and depression. Good for spine. A stone favored by musicians, as it is said to inspire them. Color: red.

SUGILITE
Uplifts and brings energy, absorbs negativity.

SUNSTONE
For contemplation, helps in remembering dreams.

TANZANITE
Helps with change, uplifts the heart.

TIGERS EYE
For good luck and protection against witchcraft and the *evil eye*. It brings insight into one's own faults and guides seekers towards right path. It is often used to help hypochondria and asthma. Color: golden brown, in bands or stripes of varying shades. Has translucent sheen associated with the cat's eye, hence the name.

TOPAZ
Believed to bring happiness, wealth and honor, improve intellect, calm the mind, and aid psychic development. For mental balance, for strengthening the blood vessels, helping circulation, varicose veins, menstrual pains, liver problems, nervousness, insomnia, and for improving appetite.

TOURMALINE
Green—helps balance and healing, best for males. Pink, helps balance and protection, best for females. It is often used in meditation. It possesses many healing properties. For cheerfulness and reconciliation, intuition, protection form enemies, negative vibrations and misfortune. Allays nervousness and brings confidence and calm. Helps clear the chakras. Used for lymphatic problems, anemia, indigestion, neuritis, weight problems, and for helping muscles and nerves. A stone favored, by artists, musicians, authors, and those in show business because it is considered a lucky stone.

TURQUOISE
(Turkish stone.) A lucky stone associated with the Buddha. It is beloved by the American Indians, and thought to bring wisdom and protection against misfortune or harm. It is considered fortunate for horses and their riders. Turquoise is said to remind us of our spiritual nature and of earthly beauty. It is often used in meditation and for assisting intuition. Good for throat chakra, higher abdomen, muscle weakness, eyes, headaches, fevers, foot, and leg problems. It encourages positive energy, and is regarded as a powerful talisman.

UNAKITE
Balances body and emotions.

ZIRCON
Promotes development of higher mind and prophecy and reduces melancholia. In healing it is used for the lungs, liver, brain, and skin problems. Color: clear or white.

Appendix Three
Essential Oils and Incenses

The Following is a basic list of properties that I have compiled. Here is a brief list of some grounding and uplifting oils and incenses that are commonly used to ground, center, and bring about a general sense of well being. Pregnant and nursing women, children, those with sensitive skin, and epileptics should use aromatherapy with extreme caution, and only under the supervision of a licensed Aromatherapist because some oils can cause extreme health complications. Please store all oils and incense away from children's reach.

AMBER
It is a calmative, analgesic, antispasmodic, expectorant, febrifuge with a warm and smoky scent and an undertone of floral citrus. Amber encourages harmony and balance, and is said to attract loving and faithful emotions. It is reported to attract prosperity and purported to transform negative energy into positive energy.

ANGELICA
A warm, musky, earthy aroma with excellent staying power. It is often used to anchor, restore, and strengthen. Also used for depression. * Avoid during pregnancy.

ANISE
Aids muscle aches, bronchitis, and indigestion. Known for its use in fisherman's soap. Said to remove human scent so that fish will be more likely to bite. It is energizing and toning, and traditionally used as a deodorant. It may induce a state of euphoria, and is used to stimulate the senses.

BALSAM PERU
Used on chafed skin to soothe. Exotic aroma, anchoring, strengthening, and imparts a rich, earthy scent to perfumes.

BASIL
It is said to be useful in stimulating healthy hair growth and may be helpful to relieve fatigue. Used in massage oil, it has a warming effect. It is used to relieve mental fatigue, to cleanse the mind, and it is said to relieve migraines.

BAY
It is often used to aid in respiratory disorders, and to relieve depression. It is reported to stimulate one's memory.

BERGAMOT
It is uplifting and refreshing. It is said to help to relieve nervous anxiety and to promote a restful sleep. Use in a diffuser as an air freshener. This oil is a skin irritant; it is best used in a diffuser.

BLUEBERRY
Burn to keep unwanted influences away from your home and property.

CALENDULA
It is said to be helpful in healing lesions and even varicose veins.

CARROT SEED
It may be useful in skin care preparations to be used on dry or mature skin.

CARNATIONS
A sweet floral scent traditionally used for healing.

CATNIP
It is used to create a psychic bond with your cat. It is often used in love sachets with rose petals. Catnip grown near the home attracts good luck and good spirits. The scent of Catnip oil is strong and not exceptionally pleasing. Studies have shown that Catnip oil is about ten times more effective than DEET for repelling mosquitoes and other insects. Blending catnip oil with Lemon Eucalyptus is said to be useful as an insect repellent, and will yield a more pleasing scent.

CEDARWOOD
Inhaled, it is believed to be helpful for respiratory conditions. It is antiseptic and fungicidal, used in a diffuser, it may kill airborne bacteria. It cleanses and purifies the body, the skin, and the environment from negativity.

CHAMOMILE
Steam distilled from the flowers with a strong, herbaceous scent. This oil gets its blue color from the content of azulene which is also anti-inflammatory in nature. Chamomile is believed to be useful for relaxation as well as beneficial in skin care.

CHERRY
Sacred to Venus, it is said that cherry will attract and stimulate love.

CINNAMON LEAF
It is a germicidal, antiseptic, and antifungal. Add a bit of cinnamon leaf, orange and clove to a diffuser or potpourri to purify the air and add a touch of warmth to your home. Strong skin irritant! Not recommended for direct application to the skin. Avoid cinnamon bark oil, as it is considered to be hazardous. Best used in a diffuser or inhaled. Used as an incense to gain wealth and success.

CITRONELLA
Steam distilled from the leaves (grass), it has a fresh, citrus scent. Citronella is commonly used to deter insects; it has a citronellal content of up to 50%. It is

also believed to be disliked by cats and may be helpful to apply to areas where you would want to deter them.

CLARY SAGE
Clary Sage is steam distilled from the flowers and leaves, the scent is grounding and herbaceous similar to Earl Grey tea. It is deeply relaxing, and it is helpful to reduce melancholy, stress and relieve tension. Clary Sage is considered by some to contain aphrodisiac qualities. Avoid use during pregnancy and avoid use after consuming alcohol as it may exaggerate the effects of alcohol.

CLEMENTINE
Steam distilled from the peel, the scent is slightly sweeter than tangerine with mild floral undertones. It is calming and relaxing, and may be useful to relieve anxiety.

CLOVE BUD
Steam distilled from the buds it is spicy, warm, and sweet. Contains antiseptic properties, and best used in a diffuser or vaporizer to help purify the air during cold and flu season. Not recommended for skin applications, it can damage skin.

COCONUT
Burn for protection and purification.

COFFEE
It is said to enhance the conscious mind.

COPAL
Sacred to the Mayan and Aztecs, this scent is suitable for honoring the Gods. It is used to uplift energies, for love, and for purification. It is burned to attract love and for purification.

CYPRESS
Steam distilled from the needles and cones, this oil has a sweet balsamic scent. It has antiseptic and astringent qualities and may be useful for respiratory conditions. It is also considered to be helpful in soothing nervous tension.

DAMIANA
Is burned to facilitate psychic visions.

DITTANY OF CRETE
It is burned to aid in astral projection and to conjure spirits.

DRAGON'S BLOOD
It is burned to dispel negativity, exorcise evil entities, enhances psychic awareness, attracts love, and is even said to restore male potency. If used at the same time with other incenses, it makes them stronger.

ELECAMPANE
It is burned to strengthen scrying abilities and clairvoyance.

EUCALYPTUS
Steam distilled from the leaves, it has a strong, camphorous odor. It is a powerful antiseptic and is highly effective when used in a vaporizer or diffuser to relieve respiratory congestion. Avoid use if you have high blood pressure or epilepsy.

EUCALYPTUS, LEMON (Eucalyptus citriodora)
This oil has a lemony scent and is useful as an insect repellent. It's antiseptic and deodorizing characteristics also makes it a nice addition to water when mopping the floor, leaving a fresh scent.

FERN
It is used as protection to exorcise evil supernatural entities. It also is purported to have rain-making properties and is said to draw luck and riches.

FIR NEEDLE
Steam distilled from the needles of the Fir tree; it has a rich, balsamic scent—the scent of an Evergreen forest. It may be useful as a respiratory tonic or to soothe anxiety.

FLAX
It is used to draw money, protection, beauty, psychic powers, and for healing.

FOXGLOVE
Is used for protection.

FRANGIAPANI
Burn to brighten your home with friendship and love.

FRANKINCENSE
There are two varieties, Boswellia carteri which is the most familiar, and Boswellia frereana. Boswellia frereana has a gentler, slightly sweet aroma. Frankincense is calming, grounding, quiets the mind, and is often used to enhance meditation. It is also said to have a restorative effect on mature and dry skin. As incense, it is used to draw upon the energy of the sun to create sacred space, consecrate objects, and stimulate positive vibrations. It is burned to dispel negativity, protect from evil, induce psychic visions, attract good luck, and to aid in meditation.

FUMITORY
It is burned to exorcise demons and evil entities.

GERANIUM
This scent is believed to have balancing and calming effects. It may be beneficial in reducing stress and anxiety and is often used for irritability associated with PMS. Many believe that its restorative and balancing properties make it useful for skin care for all skin types, especially for mature skin.

GINGER
Inhaling the scent is said to be stimulating and helpful in clearing your head. While fresh ginger root is often used as a digestive aid for upset stomach, taking

this oil internally is not recommended. Used in a compress, Ginger oil is believed to be helpful to find relief from aches and pains.

GINSENG ROOT
It is burned to keep wicked spirits away and for protection against all forms of evil.

GRAPEFRUIT
Has a fresh, citrus scent. It is refreshing and energizing, and can be used as a natural air freshener with disinfecting properties. Thought to be beneficial as an anti-depressant, as it may help relieve anxiety as well as stimulating detoxification of the body.

HELICHRYSUM
Steam distilled from the flowering tops of the plant commonly known as Immortelle, it has a distinguished scent that is vaguely tea-like, but not quite. It is believed to be exceptional in skin care with regards to bruises and scarring. Many people have claimed great success in treating scars and bruises by mixing Helichrysum with Rosehip Seed Oil. It is also said to be used to restore hearing.

HIBISCUS FLOWERS
Is burned to attract love. Hibiscus is often used in aromatherapy to treat women who have been traumatized by rape because it has a warm scent that reportedly assists women in connecting with their femininity. It is used as a muscle relaxant, diuretic, and expectorant. It also used in skin preparations to treat eczema, and improve the elasticity of the skin. It may also be found in shampoos for the treatment of dandruff, and as a moisturizer.

HONEYSUCKLE
A heavy floral scent which has an effect on salmonella and streptococcus. It can be used as an antibiotic to treat colds, flu, etc. Honeysuckle has expectorant and laxative properties. The flowers (in syrup form) have been used against diseases of the respiratory organs and in the treatment of asthma. The leaves (as a decoction) have been used to treat diseases of the liver and spleen. Honeysuckle is an herb of the mind and prosperity. When the fresh herb is rubbed on the forehead, psychic abilities are heightened. In much the same way, if Honeysuckle oil is dabbed on the temples, the person will think quicker and clearer. Honeysuckle also aids memory. Honeysuckle is an herb of devotion, fidelity and affection, and those who wear it will dream of their own true love. It is said to aid in weight loss and promotes physical flexibility. It aids in the assistance of letting go of the past, sharpening intuition, and balancing the left and right hemispheres of the brain. The incense is burned for good health, luck, and psychic power.

HOREHOUND
It is burned as an offertory incense to the Egyptian God Horus. It is often used for protection, mental powers, healing, and is used during exorcisms.

JASMINE
Is used for luck in general, especially in matters relating to love. Not recommended for women during pregnancy. This oil or incense is useful for severe depression, and for postnatal depression. On the skin, jasmine can be used to treat dry, stressed, and sensitive skins, and helps to increase elasticity. (It is often used in creams and lotions for stretch marks.) It has aphrodisiac, anti-depressant, sedative, emollient, antiseptic, and anti-spasmodic, properties.

JUNIPERBERRY
Steam distilled from the berries or a combination of berries and twigs. The scent is sweet and balsamic (similar to Gin) and the oil has antiseptic qualities. This oil may cause irritation of sensitive skin, and should be avoided by those with kidney disease.

LAVENDER
Sweet, crisp scent. It is relaxing and soothing and can be helpful in reducing stress. Many individuals use lavender to promote a blissful sleep. Powerful, yet mildly antiseptic, it can be used directly on the skin for urgent needs such as bee stings, minor cuts, and burns. Lavender is one of the best all around essential oils.

LEMON
It has a clean, refreshing and uplifting scent. Used in a diffuser, lemon will purify stale air and act as a disinfectant. Lemon juice has the ability to reduce acidity in the body and is generally beneficial to the digestive system. It stimulates the white corpuscles in the body which help to fight infection. Lemon attracts happiness and benevolent energy. May be useful to clear the mind, relieve stress, and relax muscles.

LEMONGRASS
Has a citrus aroma. It is uplifting and cleansing, and it is believed to have a sedating effect on the central nervous system. It may be effective as a natural insect repellent, but use sparingly at 1%.

LEMON VERBENA
Has a de-stressing and relaxing effect on the mind. It is useful in dealing with nervous conditions causing insomnia, and in calming heart palpitations. It helps to stimulate one's appetite, and also assists in controlling muscle spasms, cramps, indigestion, and even flatulence. Can be used on the skin to reduce puffiness, but it can be an irritant if used near the eye area. This herb is often used to treat acne, cysts, and boils. This essential oil has sedative, anti-spasmodic, aphrodisiac, bactericidal, insecticidal, antiseptic, digestive, emollient, febrifuge, hepatic, stomachic, and tonic properties. It has a positive effect on one's liver, in cases of alcohol abuse and liver damage, and it even helps to relieve bronchial and sinus congestion.

LILAC
Attracts harmony into one's life and is used to increase psychic powers.

LIME

Lime shares most of the same characteristics as lemon, including fighting infections, colds, and dyspepsia. It causes sensitivity to sunlight, so avoid exposure to the sun after direct application to the skin.

LITSEA CUBEBA

This oil has a fresh lemony, slightly floral uplifting scent similar to lemongrass, but not quite as sharp. It acts as an antiseptic, astringent, deodorant, disinfectant, insect repellant, and as a sedative.

LOTUS

For inner peace and outer harmony, to aid in meditation and to open the mind's eye. It is said that it guards against witchcraft. The ancient Greeks and Romans used it to treat asthma, internal ailments, and rheumatism. Its healing properties are reported to be helpful for epilepsy, bladder, and kidney problems, jaundice, and even the plague!

MACE

It is used to stimulate and increase psychic powers.

MASTIC

It is burned to conjure beneficial spirits, stimulate psychic powers, and to intensify sexual desires.

MANDARIN

It is a calming and relaxing oil. It is used for massage and may help prevent stretch marks. It also is used to calm the digestive system, and it is said to stimulate the appetite.

MINT

It is used to exorcise evil, to conjure beneficial spirits, and to attract money. The incense possesses extremely strong healing vibrations and protective powers.

MUGWORT

It is said to awaken psychic energies, and purify and open circulatory channels. May ease cramping and strengthen the uterus. *Avoid during pregnancy.

MUSK

Burn for courage and vitality, or to heighten sensual passion. It is used for strength and wisdom, attraction, and to heighten sexuality.

MYRRH

Myrrh has a sharp, balsamic scent. It is traditionally known for its religious uses with Frankincense. It may be useful to revitalize and nurture mature skin. Myrrh may also provide relief for bronchitis and colds when used in a diffuser or vaporizer. It is an ancient incense for protection, healing, purification, and spirituality.

NAG CHAMPA
Sacred incense of India. Good for meditation and prayer. Soothing and calming. Clears and purifies all chakras, and attracts assistance from higher realms.

NIAOULI
Steam distilled from the leaves, it has a scent similar to Tea Tree with a stronger camphorous note. It has antiseptic qualities and is believed to be beneficial for the respiratory system as well as being useful for inflammations and infections.

NUTMEG
Steam distilled from the seeds, it has the scent of freshly grated nutmeg. It is believed to have analgesic properties and may be useful in massage oil for aches and pains. It is also thought to be helpful in combating mental fatigue. Avoid large doses, as it can have a stupefying effect. To be on the safe side, avoid use during pregnancy.

OLIVE
The oil is said to revitalize all physical systems, including the mind. It is said to bring about peace of heart and mind, inspires security in love, family, and business, and assures fidelity in love, and can attract a marriage partner.

ORANGE, SWEET
Refreshing and invigorating fresh orange aroma. Its scent and properties are energizing and invigorating and may be helpful in reducing fatigue. Used as a room freshener, orange contains antiseptic qualities. Its scent may calm and soothe the nerves. Avoid direct exposure to the sun after direct application to the skin.

OREGANO
This is a potent oil which is antiseptic and kills parasites, viruses, bacteria, and fungus. Inhaled, it is believed to be beneficial for respiratory conditions that are bacterial or viral in nature. It also contains analgesic properties and works as an expectorant. * Do not use during pregnacy. Avoid direct use on skin, as it is a strong irritant, and do not ingest. (Never ingest any essential oil!)

PALMAROSA
The scent is sweet, similar to a combination of geranium and rose, with a slight citrus note. Considered to be a cellular regenerative, it may be useful in skin care preparations for dry or mature skin. It may also be useful in alleviating stress and fatigue.

PARSLEY
It may be used as purification, it is a diuretic. It aids in relieving kidney and urinary tract infections and problems, and is used to freshen breath. It is also used as a sedative and may be useful for nervous conditions. *Avoid use during pregnancy.

PATCHOULI
Intensely rich, earthy/woody scent. It contains anti-depressant properties and may be useful for relieving stress and restoring emotional balance. It works well on dry, cracked, or aging skin. It is believed by some to possess aphrodisiac qualities. An earthy scent used in money and attraction spells.

PASSIONFLOWER
For peace of mind, this sweet scent will soothe troubles and aid in sleep.

PENNYROYAL
It is useful as an insect repellent. Pennyroyal is an oral toxin—NEVER take this oil internally as it is dangerous!

PEPPERMINT
It has an energizing effect, and is often used to reduce mental fatigue and improve concentration. Peppermint aids in digestion and eases stomach upset. It may be useful to reduce pain when used in a rub, and help to reduce respiratory congestion to improve breathing. It purifies and attracts positive energies, and is beneficial for treating depression. It is said to eliminate "cobwebs" and static from the mind and the aura.

PETITGRAIN
It is uplifting and may help to reduce mental fatigue. It is mildly sedating. Petitgrain blends well with sweet scents with similar properties because it helps to balance out the fragrance. It is believed to promote restful sleep and reduce the effects of anxiety as well as helping to clear the mind. May cause sensitivity to sunlight; avoid direct exposure after direct application to the skin, use sparingly; it may cause skin irritation.

PINE NEEDLE
It is a strongly antiseptic and kills germs. It is believed to be helpful for respiratory infections as well as having a calming effect to overcome anxiety. It is often burned for strength, and to reverse negative energies.

RAVENSARA
Steam distilled from the leaves, the scent is a spicy-sweet with a slight anise-like undertone. It is believed to be useful for treating respiratory conditions, flu symptoms, and viral infections.

ROSALINA
This is a relatively new and untested oil. It is best to not use it in skin applications until more information is available. It may be useful in the diffuser for respiratory conditions.

ROSE
For love magick, and to return calm energies to the home.

ROSE OTTO
An exquisite and beautiful rose essential oil. The rose is known as the queen of flowers in Aromatherapy. It takes a very large quantity of rose petals to produce a very small amount of oil. However, this oil is extremely concentrated, so only a very small amount is needed. You may dilute rose otto in carrier oil at a rate of 10% Rose Otto to 90% carrier oil and still retain the marvelous fragrance. A combination of Rose Otto and Sandalwood is called Rose Attar and makes a wonderfully soothing and sensual blend.

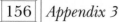

ROSEMARY

It may be helpful to reduce muscular pain when used in massage into the affected areas. It also may be help to relieve headaches when inhaled. *Avoid use if you are pregnant. There is a belief that you should avoid rosemary if you have high blood pressure or epilepsy.

ROSEWOOD

May be useful for skin care for dry, sensitive, or mature skin. This oil may also be beneficial to relieve tension and promote relaxation.

SANDALWOOD

Has a rich, woody, earthy scent that many feel contain aphrodisiac qualities. Many individuals find that sandalwood has calming and soothing effects that help reduce stress and alleviate anxiety. It is often used to enhance meditation. It has antiseptic properties which are believed to be useful for respiratory conditions. A delicious all purpose scent used to heal and protect, also for purification.

SEABUCKTHORN BERRY

It is extracted using Carbon Dioxide, rather than steam yields an oil which is truer to the essence of the plant. Seabuckthorn is rich in beta-carotene and high in vitamins A, E, and linoleic acid which makes it a wonderful oil to use in applications to soothe and restore the skin.

SPEARMINT

It is a comforting scent which can be relaxing and help to relieve mental fatigue. It is slightly antiseptic and may be useful for minor skin eruptions.

STRAWBERRY

For love, luck, and friendship. Strawberries are often served as a "love" food, and the leaves are carried for good luck.

SWEET PEA

The flowers are grown in a garden to attract friends and lovers. It is thought that bathing in the flowers will increase one's popularity.

TANGERINE

It is uplifting and refreshing and may help to soothe troubling emotions. Its scent often has a calming and sedating effect and may help to ease nervous tension. May cause sensitivity to sunlight, avoid exposure to direct sun for six hours after direct application to the skin. It is a possible skin irritant, always dilute in carrier oil. A solar aroma used to attract prosperity

TEA TREE

It is a powerful, yet gentle antiseptic and disinfectant. Often used for the treatment of athlete's foot. Can be used directly on cuts to cleanse and disinfect. Works well for soothing itching caused by insect bites. Works well applied directly to pimples. This is exceptional oil and one of the few that is acceptable to use directly on the skin, although dilution is recommended.

THYME
Contains antiviral and antibacterial properties. Kills airborne bacteria when used in a vaporizer or diffuser, and may provide relief of symptoms from bronchitis or pneumonia. Skin irritant!

VANILLA
It may be used to stimulate amorous appetites and enhance memory and mental powers.

VERVAIN
It may be used to bring about love, protection, purification, peace, money, youth, chastity, sleep, and healing properties.

VETIVERT
It stimulates circulation and helps to relieve joint pain and arthritis. It is relaxing and said to reduce blood pressure. It is said to induce love, and is hex breaking, and encourages luck and money, and is even considered to have anti-theft properties.

VIOLET
The Ancient Greeks wore violet as a symbol of fertility and to induce sleep. It may be used for protection and luck in love, and to bring about peace and healing.

WORMWOOD
It is said to stimulate psychic powers, and is used for protection, love, and calling spirits. It has been used for centuries as a moth repellant, general pesticide, and as a tea/spray to repel slugs and snails. Historic references to wormwood go back as far as 1600 B.C. in Egypt. Wormwood leaves contain absinthin, a substance which is toxic to other plants. (The alcoholic drink "absinthe" is a green-colored beverage that is now illegal in most countries. It has been said that the painter Vincent van Gogh was imbibing of absinthe when he cut off his ear to send to a woman.)

YARROW
It is useful for severe skin rashes and wounds that will not heal; it acts as an anti-inflammatory. It is useful for calming nerves, lowering blood pressure, for insomnia, and stress related problems.
* Avoid if Pregnant! It should not be used on Children under ten years of age.

YLANG YLANG
It is very seductive scent, and believed to possess aphrodisiac qualities. It is a re-laxing and soothing scent that may help to relieve anxiety and calm the nervous system. It is often used for promoting a restful sleep.

Appendix Four
Tools of the Paranormal Trade

Today, there are quite a few tools of the paranormal trade. EMF Detectors measure the level of electromagnetic fields in an area. If you look online, you may find a plethora of instruments called "ghost detectors." Essentially what these are: EMF and ELF Detectors; they are devices that measure the magnetic and the electric levels in the surrounding area.

Please keep in mind that these detectors will "go off" if you are near a power source, such as an electrical outlet, a fuse box, or near any major power source. If the detector is going past seven, chances are you are near a power source. True paranormal activity generally falls in the range of a two to a six.

Sometimes there are no readings on an EMF or ELF detector when there *is* paranormal activity, which leads many to believe that the atmosphere is being changed by the spiritual in much more than on an electromagnetic field. In essence we are looking for changes in the atmosphere that surrounds us; there is no true "Ghost Detector."

This leads us to using a lot of really cool gadgets which fall under the category of weather instruments. Inherently, we use weather instruments. An Air Probe Thermometer uses an external probe which is capable of taking measurements in the air temperature. This instrument is extremely handy when there is a flux in temperature whether it drops or increases. Which brings me to another strange phenomenon which is "cold spots; " these "cold spots" occur much for the same reason that batteries drain; an energy is attempting to manifest, and it is thought that the energy is drawing from the surrounding fields in the atmosphere. Other instruments used include a compass, which was used by early paranormal investigators to detect an anomalous field. Nowadays, you can get cool digital thermometers which give digital readings of time, and temperature, as well.

When we conduct an investigation, we use analog and digital voice recorders, digital cameras, 35mm cameras, and video cameras. We record the current time, temperature, and all of our normal speaking voices into the recorders before we begin an EVP session. (As mentioned earlier, an EVP is Electronic Voice Phenomena.) We take as many photos as possible. We are meticulous about going through all of our evidence, and log everything.

When we come across a photo that has an orb, we look at it very carefully. Orbs are anomalous spherical shapes that appear on video and still photography. Because of the advent of digital photography, more and more orbs are appearing in photographs. What is happening is the result of the pixelization within the photo. The higher the megapixels a camera has, the better the quality photo and less filling in of pixels. When taking photos with a lower megapixel camera, such as a 3.0, the quality of the photo begins to diminish due to pixelazation.

Ideally, 35mm cameras are the best, or digital cameras above a 5.0. It is best to use the highest quality you can, such as a RAW or TIFF format. A photo is compressed each time you open and close it on your computer; what this means is, the photo loses some of its detail and quality.

Another thing to look for when looking at an orb: moisture and dust in the air, and light sources. An orb is an orb no matter which way you look at it, but it is good to take a look carefully and analyze the photograph before jumping to any conclusions that you indeed have a "spirit" caught on film.

There are other pieces of equipment which may be used to detect other changes in the atmosphere, such as a Geiger Counter which measures gamma and x-ray radiation, and Infra Red which is an invisible band of radiation at the lower end of the visible light spectrum. With wavelengths from 750 nm to 1 mm, infrared starts at the end of the microwave spectrum and ends at the beginning of visible light. Infrared transmission typically requires an unobstructed line of sight between transmitter and receiver. Widely used in most audio and video remote controls, infrared transmission is also used for wireless connections between computer devices and a variety of detectors. There are Infra Red Cameras, but they are expensive.

We are usually requested to do an investigation or we ask permission when we go to public areas such as Fort Mifflin, and Eastern State Penitentiary. We never break and enter, and we always remain respectful to our hosts, surroundings, and teammates. (We ask that you do the same.) Paranormal investigation is definitely a team effort. No one person can hold all of these contraptions, unless you have eight arms such as The Goddess Mahapratisara (A Tibetan eight-armed deity with four faces), not that anyone needs four faces, but it would definitely be an advantage as far as investigating paranormal phenomenon goes. The field of paranormal research is growing and becoming much more scientific in nature. There is still a lot to learn and research about ghostly phenomena.

The proceeding chapters regarding gemstones and essential oils and incense was requested, in fact, by my editor. The nature of paranormal phenomena is a spiritual source which is still being investigated, and to this day remains unknown. Therefore, as paranormal investigators we use our own spiritual beliefs and other methods to keep us grounded and safe during an investigation. Since we all have different religious beliefs there is no one single method, except for staying strong in one's faith. Whatever ones faith is, it is important to believe in its power to keep one strong and safe from harm. Some of us carry gemstones and wear talismans, some of us pray or use mantras, some of us use essential oils and incense before and after an investigation. Whatever works, works.

Appendix Five
Clairvoyants and Mediums

A lot of psychics, clairvoyants, and mediums have been making their way on to television and the media. Some are the real thing, some remain questionable at best. I have been blessed with finding only a few with true talent. One has guided me on my path and has been an inspiring person to me.

When I first moved to Philadelphia, I was in the throes of a nasty divorce and I was extremely upset and confused. While waiting in line at a local store, I met an amazing woman. She was comforting her child, who was unfortunately sick. I was just done with work and ready to make my trek back home, but somehow I was fascinated by this young mother. She looked at me and smiled and said, "Please don't think I'm weird, but I'd like to talk to you about something."

I said, "Okay…" I thought she was about to ask me for money. She did not ask me for money. As we began to walk out of the store, she said to me, "You must stay strong; there are powerful energies working for you, please believe me…"

I remained skeptical, but intrigued. She began to divulge some things which I had never told anyone, and even had a difficult time admitting to myself. She asked me to sit down with her for a moment, and I did. She introduced me to gemstones to hold on to, and she explained that they were just for me to handle. She asked for no money at all, and sent me on my way with a blessing saying, "the light will guide you and protect you in all of your endeavors." I was told that something wonderful was coming. And it did—more quickly than I'd anticipated!

I happened to meet an amazing person, and I happened to find myself at 5:30 am on the set of *12 Monkeys* as an extra the very next day. The intriguing and mysterious lady who I wanted to run and thank had disappeared, her shop was not there, and she was gone.

Throughout my life, I have been in contact with mediums and psychics. Unfortunately, there are scam artists out there whom I have run across, so please be aware and be careful. The genuine ones are amazing and you know when you've found one. I have been informed by a reputable source that I have "gifts." Needless to say, I am a quirky person. I had been going to therapy for years and was put on some massive medications, but regrettably, all they did was turn me into a "stupid zombie face" as I like to say. "Mmmm, Gimme brains...." Seriously, it is an interesting and odd "gift" I have. I have begun to understand it more, although it still feels a bit unusual to actually put it into practice.

The most important thing for me is still to remain skeptical as a paranormal investigator. However, I must admit that it is fascinating to find out that I am right about someone or something... Even psychics use tools such as dowsing rods which are a pair of L-shaped rods or a single Y-shaped rod, which are used to detect the presence of an anomalous energy, or in other words a "spirit." Sometimes pendulums are utilized—these are a pointed item, usually a crystal or an ingot, that is hung on the end of a string or chain and is used as a means of contacting spirits. An individual will hold the item and let it hang from the finger tips. That person will ask questions aloud and the pendulum answers by moving.

Another form of contacting spirits includes table tipping, which is the act of a table being used as a form of contact. Individuals will sit around a table, lightly place their fingertips on the edge of the table, and elicit contact with a spirit. The Spirit will respond by "tipping" or moving the table. Even talking boards are used, but I strongly advise against the use of these items, also known as a Ouija Board™. A board is used as a means of communicating with a spirit. Mediums are able to pick up on a spirit's presence in a room. Not all mediums are alike; some pick up on audible sounds and visions, or impressions. Some have dreams which are oddly prophetic. Sensitivity to spirits can include the feeling of literally being nauseous, like the room is spinning, and obviously, if one sees something or hears something that others do not.

Children are the most open to being sensitive due to their naivety and youth. This "gift" is not something to just play with. Unfortunately, due to the nature of these "gifts," some people are institutionalized. Others are taunted and picked on by skeptics. Skeptics are good; they keep everything in balance. However, it is unnecessary to be cruel in one's skepticism. Due to the nature of our work as investigators, we have fielded some rather rude skeptics who say that we need to "get a life" or "get a real job"—or worse.

Truth be told, I have a few jobs, and barely have time to devote what I would like to paranormal research, and just barely make enough money to get by. I am by no means a psychic and do not wish to be called one. I do not do readings, and, in fact, I am incredibly, extremely-shy and quirky! I do seem to be a magnet for "odd occurrences" as some of my friends like to say...

Quite often clairvoyants run séances, which are small groups of no more than eight people. Large groups generally do not work well. The first few séances date as far back as the third century C.E. in the writings of Porphyry. In 1659, *A True and Faithful Relation of What Passed Between Dr. Dee and Some Spirits*, one of the first recorded séances is recorded, which is written by Reverend Meric Casaubon.

The Fox twins caused an amazing phenomenon in stirring the spiritualist movement. Both Catherine and Margaretta Fox became extremely famous for conversing with a ghost haunting their home in Hydesville, New York. They used a series of rapping noises to communicate with the ghost which inhabited their home.

Unfortunately, not all séances are successful. Sometimes the sitters in a séance may be disappointed if certain results are expected. Sometimes one's very desperation to contact to a loved one that has passed can cause this situation of being incredibly disappointed.

The one thing that I, skeptics, and Social Scientists can agree on: It is rather obvious when someone is a Sociopath or Schizophrenic due to psychological disturbances, and they, on the other hand, do require proper treatment. The use of Mediums is becoming much more prevalent in law enforcement. Alison DuBois, the famed medium (who by the way refuses to be called a psychic because of the negative connotation), upon which the television show *The Medium* is based upon, appears to be the real deal. She has been assisting law enforcement in Arizona and has had accurate and startling results.

Summing things up, I believe that as more people become in touch with themselves, and more interested in the paranormal side of life, an intuitive nature will become available to everyone in some fashion.

Conclusion

Whether you are interested in the history of Philadelphia— ghost or otherwise— or just want to spend your time at some lively (and often frightening) ghost locations, Philly has a haunt for you!

It was a fascinating day touring the cemetery.
Photo by Katharine Sarro

Glossary

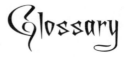

* The following section is provided by the Chester County Paranormal Research Society in Pennsylvania and appears in training materials for new investigators. Please visit www.ChesterCountyprs.com for more information.

Air Probe Thermometer
A thermometer with an external probe that is capable of taking instant measurements of the air temperature.

Anomalous field
A field that can not be explained or ruled out by various possibilities, that can be a representation of spirit or paranormal energy present.

Apparition
A transparent form of a human or animal, a spirit.

Artificial field
A field that is caused by electrical outlets, appliances, etc.

Aural Enhancer
A listening device that enhances or amplifies audio signals. i.e., Orbitor Bionic Ear.

Automatic writing
The act of a spirit guiding a human agent in writing a message that is brought through by the spirit.

Base readings
The readings taken at the start of an investigation and are used as a means of comparing other readings taken later during the course of the investigation.

Demonic Haunting
A haunting that is caused by an inhuman or subhuman energy or spirit.

Dowsing Rods

A pair of L-shaped rods or a single Y-shaped rod, used to detect the presence of what the person using them is trying to find.

Electro-static generator

A device that electrically charges the air often used in paranormal investigations/research as a means to contribute to the materialization of paranormal or spiritual energy.

ELF

Extremely Low Frequency.

ELF Meter/EMF Meter

A device that measures electric and magnetic fields.

EMF

Electro Magnetic Field.

EVP

Electronic Voice Phenomena.

False positive

Something that is being interpreted as paranormal within a picture or video and is, in fact, a natural occurrence or defect of the equipment used.

Gamera

A 35mm film camera connected with a motion detector that is housed in a weather proof container and takes a picture when movement is detected. Made by Silver Creek Industries.

Geiger Counter

A device that measures gamma and x-ray radiation.

Infra Red

An invisible band of radiation at the lower end of the visible light spectrum. With wavelengths from 750 nm to 1 mm, infrared starts at the end of the microwave spectrum and ends at the beginning of visible light. Infrared transmission typically requires an unobstructed line of sight between transmitter and receiver. Widely used in most audio and video remote controls, infrared transmission is also used for wireless connections between computer devices and a variety of detectors.

Intelligent haunting

A haunting of a spirit or other entity that has the ability to interact with the living and do things that can make its presence known.

Milli-gauss

Unit of measurement, measures in 1000th of a gauss and is named for the famous German mathematician, Karl Gauss.

Orbs

Anomalous spherical shapes that appear on video and still photography.

Pendulum

A pointed item that is hung on the end of a string or chain and is used as a means of contacting spirits. An individual will hold the item and let it hang from the finger tips. The individual will ask questions aloud and the pendulum answers by moving.

Poltergeist haunting

A haunting that has two sides, but same kinds of activity in common. Violent outbursts of activity with doors and windows slamming shut, items being thrown across a room and things being knocked off of surfaces. Poltergeist hauntings are usually focused around a specific individual who resides or works at the location of the activity reported, and, in some cases, when the person is not present at the location, activity does not occur. A poltergeist haunting may be the cause of a human agent or spirit/energy that may be present at the location.

Portal

An opening in the realm of the paranormal that is a gateway between one dimension and the next. A passageway for spirits to come and go through. See also Vortex.

Residual haunting

A haunting that is an imprint of an event or person that plays itself out like a loop until the energy that causes it has burned itself out.

Scrying

The act of eliciting information with the use of a pendulum from spirits.

Table Tipping

A form of spirit communication, the act of a table being used as a form of contact. Individuals will sit around a table and lightly place their fingertips on the edge of the table and elicit contact with a spirit. The Spirit will respond by "tipping" or moving the table.

Talking Boards

A board used as a means of communicating with a spirit. Also known as a Quija Board™.

Vortex

A place or situation regarded as drawing into its center all that surrounds it.

White Noise

A random noise signal that has the same sound energy level at all frequencies.

Equipment Explanations

In this section, the Chester County Paranormal Research Society looks at the application and benefits of equipment used on investigations with greater detail. The equipment used for an investigation plays a vital role in the ability to collect objective evidence and helps to determine what *is* and *is not* paranormal activity. But a key point to be made here is: the investigator is the most important tool on any investigation. With that said, let us now take a look at the main pieces of equipment used during an investigation…

The Geiger Counter

The Geiger counter is device that measures radiation. A "Geiger counter" usually contains a metal tube with a thin metal wire along its middle. The space in between them is sealed off and filled with a suitable gas and with the wire at about +1000 volts relative to the tube.

An ion or electron penetrating the tube (or an electron knocked out of the wall by X-rays or gamma rays) tears electrons off atoms in the gas. Because of the high positive voltage of the central wire, those electrons are then attracted to it. They gain energy that collide with atoms and release more electrons, until the process snowballs into an "avalanche", producing an easily detectable pulse of current. With a suitable filling gas, the flow of electricity stops by itself, or else the electrical circuitry can help stop it.

The instrument was called a "counter" because every particle passing it produced an identical pulse, allowing particles to be counted, usually electronically. But it did not tell anything about their identity or energy, except that they must have sufficient energy to penetrate the walls of the counter.

The Geiger counter is used in paranormal research to measure the background radiation at a location. The working theory in this field is that paranormal activity can effect the background radiation. In some cases, it will increase the radiation levels and in other cases it will decrease the levels.

Digital and 35mm Film Cameras

The camera is an imperative piece of equipment that enabled us to gather objective evidence during a case. Some of the best evidence presented from cases of paranormal activity over the years has been because of photographs taken. If you own your own digital camera or 35mm film camera, you need to be fully aware of what the cameras abilities and limitations are. Digital cameras have been at the center of great debate in the field of paranormal research over the years.

The earlier incarnations of digital cameras were full of inherent problems and notorious for creating "false positive" pictures. A "false positive" picture is a picture that has anomalous elements within the picture that are the result of a camera defect or other natural occurrence. There are many pictures scattered about the internet that claim to be of true paranormal activity, but in fact they are "false positives." Orbs, defined as anomalous paranormal energy that can show up as balls of light or streaks in still photography or video, are the most controversial pictures of paranormal energy in the field. There are so many theories (good and bad) about the origin of orbs and what they are. Every picture in the CCPRS collection that has an orb—or orbs—are not presented in a way that state that they are absolutely paranormal of nature. I have yet to capture an orb photo that made me feel certain that in fact it is of a paranormal nature.

If you use your own camera, understand that your camera is vital. I encourage all members who own their own cameras to do research on the make and model of the camera and see what other consumers are saying about them. Does the manufacturer give any info regarding possible defects or design flaws with that particular model? Understanding your camera will help to rule out the possibility of interpreting a "false positive" for an authentic picture of paranormal activity.

Video Cameras

The video camera is also a fundamental tool in the investigation as another way for collecting objective evidence that can support the proof of paranormal activity. The video camera can be used in various ways during the investigation. It can be set on a tripod and left in a location where paranormal activity has been reported. It can also be used as a hand-held camera and the investigator will take it with them during their walk through investigation as a means of documenting to hopefully capture anomalous activity on tape. Infra-Red technology has become a feature on most consumer level video cameras and depending on the manufacturer can be called "night shot" or "night alive." What this technology does is allow us to use the camera in zero light. Most cameras with this feature will add a green tint or haze to the camera when it is being used in this mode. A video camera with this ability holds great appeal to the paranormal investigator.

EMF/ELF Meters

EMF=Electro Magnetic Frequency
ELF=Extremely Low Frequency

What is an EMF/ELF meter? Good question. The EMF/ELF meter is a meter that measures Electric and Magnetic fields in an AC or DC current field. It measures in a unit of measurement called "milli-gauss," named for the famous German mathematician, Karl Gauss. Most meters will measure in a range of 1-5 or 1-10 milli-gauss. The reason that EMF meters are used in paranormal research is because of the theory that a spirit or paranormal energy can add to the energy field when it is materializing or is present in a location. The theory says that, typically, an energy that measures between 3-7 milli-gauss may be of a paranormal origin. This doesn't mean that an artificial field can't also measure within this range. That is why we take base readings and make maps notating where artificial fields occur. The artificial fields are a direct result of electricity, i.e. wiring, appliances, light switches, electrical outlets, circuit breakers, high voltage power lines, sub-stations, etc.

The Earth emits a naturally occurring magnetic field all around us and has an effect on paranormal activity. Geo-magnetic storm activity can also have a great influence on paranormal activity. For more information on this kind of phenomena visit: www.noaa.sec.com.

There are many different types of EMF meters; and each one, although it measures with the same unit of measurement, may react differently. An EMF meter can range from anywhere to $12.00 to $1,000.00 or more depending on the quality and features that it has. Most meters are measuring the AC (alternating current, the type of fields created by man-made electricity) fields and some can measure DC (direct current-naturally occurring fields, batteries also fall into the category of DC) fields. The benefit of having a meter that can measure DC fields is that they will automatically filter out the artificial fields created by AC fields and can pick up more naturally occurring electro magnetic fields. Some of the higher-tech EMF meters are so sensitive that they can pick up the fields generated by living beings. The EMF meter was originally designed to measure the earth's magnetic fields and also to measure the fields created by electrical an artificial means.

There have been various studies over the years about the long term effects of individuals living in or near high fields. There has been much controversy as to whether or not long term exposure to high fields can lead to cancer. It has been proven though that no matter what, long term exposure to high fields can be harmful to your health. The ability to locate these high fields within a private residence or business is vital to the investigation. We may offer suggestions to the client as to possible solutions for dealing with high fields. The wiring in a home or business can greatly affect the possibility of high fields. If the wiring is old and/or not shielded correctly, it can emit high fields that may affect the ability to correctly notate any anomalous fields that may be present.

Audio Recording Equipment

Audio recording equipment is used for conducting EVP (Electronic Voice Phenomena) research and experiments. What is an EVP? An EVP is a phenomenon where paranormal voices or sounds can be captured with audio recording devices. The theory is that the activity will imprint directly onto the device or tape, but has not been proven to be an absolute fact. The use of an external microphone is essential when conducting EVP experiments with analog recording equipment. The internal microphone on an analog tape recorder can pick up the background noise of the working parts within the tape recorder and can taint the evidence as a whole. Most digital recorders are quiet enough to use the internal microphone, but as a general rule of thumb, we do not use them. An external microphone will be used always. Another theory about EVP research is that an authentic EVP will happen within the range 250-400hz. This is a lower frequency range and isn't easily heard by the human ear, and the human voice does not emit in this range. EVP is rarely heard at the moment it happens—it is usually revealed during the playback and analysis portion of the investigation.

Thermometers

The use of a thermometer in an investigation goes without saying. This is how we monitor the temperature changes during the course of an investigation. CCPRS is currently using Digital thermometers with remote sensors as a way to set up a perimeter and to notate any changes in a stationary location of an investigation. The Air-probe thermometer can take "real time" readings that are instantly accurate. This is the more appropriate thermometer for measuring air temperature and "cold spots" that may be caused by the presence of paranormal phenomena. The IR Non-contact thermometer is the most misused thermometer in the field of paranormal research. CCPRS does not own or use IR Non-contact thermometers for this reason. The IR (infra-red) Non-contact thermometer is meant for measuring surface temperatures from a remote location. It shoots an infrared beam out to an object and bounces to the unit and gives the temperature reading. I have seen, first hand, investigators using this thermometer as a way to measure air temperature. NO, this is not correct! Enough said. In an email conversation that I have had with Grant Wilson from TAPS, he has said that, "Any change in temperature that can't be measured with your hand is not worth notating…"

Bibliography

Books

Adams III, Charles J. *Philadelphia Ghost Stories*. Reading, PA: Exeter House Books, 2001

Asfar, Dan. *Ghost Stories of Pennsylvania*. Edmonton, Canada: Ghost House Books, 2002.

Cunningham, Scott. *Cunningham's Encyclopedia of Crystal, Gem, & Metal Magic*. St. Paul, MN: Llewellyn Publications, 1988.

Guiley, Rosemary Ellen. *The Encyclopedia of Ghosts and Spirits Second Edition*. New York, New York: Visionary Living, Inc, 2000.

Hull, Laurie. *Brandywine Valley Ghosts: Chadds Ford, Concordville, Thorton, and Media*. Atglen, PA: Schiffer Publishing, Ltd., 2008.

Knight, Sirona. *Pocket Guide to Crystals & Gemstones*. Freedom, CA: The Crossing Press, 1998.

Lake, Matt. *Weird Pennsylvania*. New York: Sterling Publishing Co., 2005.

Mack, Carol K. & Dinah Mack. *A Field Guide to Demons, Fairies, Fallen Angels, And Other Subversive Spirits*. New York: Henry Holt and Company, 1998.

Taylor, Troy. *Field Guide to Haunted Graveyards*. Alton, IL: Whitechapel Productions Press, 2003.

Video

Let the Doors be of Iron, Hal Kirn & Associates
Voices of Eastern State, Hal Kirn & Associates

Individuals and Organizations

CCPRS—Chester County Paranormal Research Society,
Anonymous Sources,
Eastern State Penitentiary,
Fort Mifflin,
Peter Hoge,
Maureen Lynch,
ECHO-Christine Gentry-Rodriguez and Jack Rodriguez,
Dinah Roseberry

Internet

http://pagans.wordpress.com/herbs-incense-and-stones/
http://philadelphia.about.com/cs/halloween/a/haunted_phila.htm
http://philadelphia.about.com/cs/halloween/a/haunted_phila_2.htm
http://rahe.org/signatura/index_files/Page387.htm
http://www.aromathyme.com/essentialoils4.html
http://www.bellbookandcandle.citymaker.com/page/page/1284328.htm
http://www.creativewomensnetwork.co.uk/gemstoneproperties.htm
http://www.easternstate.org
http://www.emeraldgypsy.com/z_herb_properties.html
http://www.essential7.com/essentialoils/lotus.html
http://www.fortmifflin.us/
http://www.fortunecity.com/lavender/strangelove/197/page8.html
http://www.ghorganics.com/Wormwood.html
http://www.ghosthunterstore.com/
http://www.haunted-places.com/misc_states/HAUNT_PA.htm
http://www.moorestownghostresearch.com/Cases/FortMifflin/FortMifflin.html
http://www.mysterynet.com/edgar-allan-poe/
http://www.nonet.net/ghosts/candleherbs.htm
http://www.philadelphiaweekly.com/view.php?id=13063
http://www.rodneyanonymous.com/radio/mifflin.html
http://www.theherbgoddess.com/Hibiscus_Flower_p/2390.htm
http://www.unsolvedmysteries.com/usm60103.html
http://www.ushistory.org/betsy/flaghome.html

Index of Places